NETWORKING IN LIBRARY SCIENCE

PREFACE

The network concept includes the development of cooperative systems of libraries on geographical, subject, or other lines, each with some kind of center that not only coordinates the internal activities of the system but also serves as the system's outlet to, and inlet from, the centers of other systems. The concept is also hierarchical in that the centers of smaller systems are channels to centers of larger networks at state, national, and even international levels.

The concept of networking is interwired with the history of interlibrary loan. Early sponsors of interlibrary loan described it without calling it by name. Networking began to develop on a national scale with the activities of the LC.

Other factors accelerated the trend toward networks. The quantity of materials being published is only one of them. In the past, libraries served their patrons from their own collections as much as possible, using interlibrary loan as a supplement.

There are very few libraries in the India now that do not belong to some sort of network, either formal or informal. Public library systems represent a particular type of cooperation. Within a given geographic region, public libraries may join together to establish and maintain a union catalog in order to provide information for patrons using a library in another part of the geographic region. This type of agreement is often accompanied by a delivery mechanism.

Many libraries belong to more than one network, taking advantage of the various services of each. Libraries may belong to a local network and a state network; they may also belong to a regional or national network.

Union catalogs, made available through networks, have made possible the "extended library." Individuals or libraries can use on-line terminals to identify a book, its location, and, in some cases, its availability.

Editor

CONTENTS

1

Networking

In the past, the library community and the academic computing community have used the *word network* to describe two different phenomena. To the computing community, a network is a general-purpose structure that links computers and supports a wide range of activities. It is like a highway system, providing a basic facility, a means to get from one place to another. Library networks, however, are organizations that provide high-level services such as shared cataloging or interlibrary loan; these services usually are based on a computer network of some sort, but the justification for a library network is the service it provides, not the communication facility itself.

A network may be thought to as either a formal or an informal linkage of discrete library units and other information-dispensing agencies for the purpose of exchanging or transferring recorded information. Exchanging and transferring is emphasized, implying two-way communication and some sort of switching mechanism.

Networks may be used for various cooperative ventures cataloging and processing, reference services, collection development, resource sharing, and others. The ILL function is dependent on efficient methods of transmission of requests and document delivery. Whenever a group of libraries can agree on a formal procedure of transmission and delivery, improvement in service is almost always reached. Ron Miller stated that, at the very least, a self-respecting network should have plans for computerization even though it can call itself a network if a delivery system or regional ILL arrangement has been agreed upon.

The network concept includes the development of cooperative systems of libraries on geographical, subject, or other lines, each with some kind of center that not only coordinates the internal activities of the system but also serves as the system's outlet to, and inlet from, the centers of other systems. The concept is also hierarchical in that the centers of smaller systems are channels to centers of larger networks at state, national, and even international levels.

Why Networking

One of the most common types of traditional networks is the ILL network in which groups of libraries agree to provide lending privileges to each other; this agreement often contains a mechanism to identify holdings to facilitate lending and borrowing.

The concept of networking is interwired with the history of interlibrary loan. Early sponsors of interlibrary loan described it without calling it by name. Networking began to develop on a national scale with the activities of the LC. The communication mechanism, or location tool, was born in 1901 when the LC began producing and distributing catalog cards. Resource sharing exploded when the LC again led the way by designing and then receiving national and international acceptance of the MARC format. It began distributing these data in 1969.

Other factors accelerated the trend toward networks. The quantity of materials being published is only one of them. In the past, libraries served their patrons from their own collections as much as possible, using interlibrary loan as a supplement. Decreasing purchasing power and increasing service to patrons have caused libraries to view a collection as being not only materials owned by an individual library but materials owned by other libraries as well.

Types of Communication

(1) Tele Type: In 1927, the Free Library of Philadelphia used a teletypewriter as part of a closed circuit to communicate information from the loan desk in the main reading room to and from the stacks. In the 1940s, Michigan librarians connected two different city libraries with a teletypewriter.

The result of a fire in the Michigan State Library was the installation of a teletype circuit typing together the resources of most of the major libraries in Michigan. Each of the libraries paid the charges for its own requests. The teletype was used for other purposes as well, but its ability to improve library cooperation and speed interlibrary loans so inspired librarians that they encouraged others to install teletype machines. It was reported in 1968 that a "hot line" teletype system, coupled with a speedy delivery system, was being used by Western Michigan University libraries to get interlibrary loans to their extension students.

The system used in the state of Louisiana, the Louisiana Rapid Communications System, combined the features of the TWX and the Wide Area Telecommunications Service (WATS) in a manner providing each library in the state with almost instantaneous communication with any other library in Louisiana, using the state library as a relay station. Even with such rapid communication available, however, Kleiner reported that the system was slow to catch on. Some libraries lost their machines because they used them. So seldom that the cost per transaction was prohibitive. Many continued to place requests via mail, although a TWX or WATS number was available to them.

The Texas State Library Communication Network began in 1968. Administration of the network was the responsibility of the state library. It and major resource center libraries were compensated by LSCA (Library Services and Construction Act) funds. When an area library could not fill requests from its community libraries, these and its own requests were referred to its major resource center library. If that library was unable to comply, the requests were referred to the Texas State Library. If it did not own the material, it sent the request to the other major resource center libraries or (for scholarly materials) to the University of Texas at Austin.

In every stage of a transaction there was both downward and upward activity-downward when a borrowing library's request could be filled and upward to a library with greater resources if a request could not be filled. As a request progressed upward, resources became greater and the possibility of its being filled increased. The community, area, and major resource libraries communicated by telephone; the major resource center libraries and the Texas State Library communicated by teletype.

The Iowa Library Information Teletype Exchange (I-LITE), begun in 1969, noted that a filled request might cost as much as $5.21. The greatest problem was the length of time required for the requests to make a complete circuit and for unfilled requests to be returned to originating libraries.

Upon the advice of its consultant, the Montana State Library replaced its TWX equipment with microprocessor-based equipment in order to save money and speed up ILL transactions. The software package selected to format, edit, and transmit ILL requests was MicroCourier, developed by MicroCom.

MicroCourier allows the operator to prepare and edit interlibrary loan requests during working hours and send them automatically during evening hours, when telephone rates are lower. The microcomputer also acts like a computer terminal to send messages to libraries that subscribe to the Ontyme II electronic mail (E-mail) service and to interact with other host computers like Montana University system computers.

The microcomputer systems were installed in 1981 at the Montana State Library and at the headquarters buildings of six public libraries. Batches of requests are sent in round robin fashion. As many requests as possible are filled in-state before being sent to out-of-state libraries. By the time a request reaches the last stop, it will have been checked against the holdings of four public libraries, two university libraries, and the state library. The state library checks the remaining requests against the Western Library Network (WLN) database.

It was found that the microcomputers functioned with more ease and speed than did the TWX machines, even through there were drawbacks with the software, which is basically a business application package. Telecommuni-cation costs were considerably less for microcomputers than for TWX-about $.20 per request for microcomputer-to-microcomputer transmission compared to over $1.25 per request for TWX machine operation.

(2) Telefacsimile: Librarians began experimenting with telefacsimile, or fax, in the 1960s, using it mainly to send interlibrary loan requests and brief journal articles. The early machines required up to six minutes to transmit one page of text: The equipment was expensive and unreliable, produced low-quality copies, and was not serviced by its manufacturers. It also did not always reduce the time involved in document delivery. Most of the networks that used fax only for communicating the actual loan requests replaced the systems with TWX or telephone.

In 1978 TALINET (Telefax Library Information Network) was designed to access the use of fax in document delivery to remote communities in Colorado, Kansas, Montana, Wyoming, and South Dakota. The study concluded that the technology was suitable, but the cost was still too high in light of the limited demand for that kind of service.

In 1981, when high-speed digital fax machines were becoming available, another study concluded that fax was still not very successful due to expense, staff time, and the need to improve the technology. Since the mid-1980s, however, interest has increased and a variety of studies and projects conducted in the Denver Public Library, Texas A&M University's College of Medicine, the Western Council of State Libraries, New York and Columbia universities, Texas College of Osteopathic Medicine, the National Library of Canada, and the College of Physician of Philadelphia indicate librarian and user satisfaction.

Pennsylvania libraries installed fax equipment to speed document delivery. Requests may still be placed through bibliographic utilities. Protocols and guidelines were drawn up to supplement procedures outlined in ILL codes. The ALA form is used for requests sent by fax rather than through bibliographic utilities. Subject requests are sent only to those libraries with whom a prior agreement has been made.

So extensive is the fax network that publications have been written on the applications of fax in libraries, comparisons of E-mail and fax, telecommunication costs, ILL guidelines, and directories of fax numbers. Two such publications. The Automotive Guide on the Use of Telefacsimile in libraries and Telefacsimile Directory of Ohio Libraries. Directories of fax numbers are available for the Rocky Mountain area (Action for Libraries), for the New England area (Directory of FAX Numbers in New England Libraries), and, indeed, for the entire North American area (Directory of Telefacsimile Sites in North American Libraries).

(3) Computer: The by-product of on-line shared cataloging was the ability to verify and transmit interlibrary loans on-line. Automated ILL systems exist in every major bibliographic utility.

The successful on-line network requires a significant level of financial and organizational commitment from participants; it is based upon agreement within the group of participants that specific tasks should be performed and specific guidelines adhered to; and it provides an immediate facility for access, through computer and communications technologies, to databases that may stem from both the public and private sectors of the information community. Because involvement entails a sizable financial commitment, representing both direct and indirect costs, libraries that are network participants must actively use the network's services in order to derive benefits commensurate with their levels of expenditure.

In the United States, the 1960s was a period of affluence compared to the leaner years of the 1970s, when funds to start new projects or to expand those already begun were limited. During the 1970s, there were fewer systems for automating the ope'ations of a single institution. Efforts were concentrated on building systems to use a single computer-based file to serve the processing and public service needs to many institutions.

Since the advent of the automated library network in the 1970s, it is no longer easy to distinguish between the traditional network and the computerized network. The traditional network has changed to meet modern needs. Working concluded that the introduction of on-line library automation into liberal arts college libraries lagged behind the same phenomenon in the ARL libraries, but automation caught on rapidly with this group during the 1980s.

There are very few libraries in the United States now that do not belong to some sort of network, either formal or informal. Public library systems represent a particular type of cooperation. Within a given geographic region, public libraries may join together to establish and maintain a union catalog in order to provide information for patrons using a library in another part of the geographic region. This type of agreement is often accompanied by a delivery mechanism.

Many libraries belong to more than one network, taking advantage of the various services of each. Libraries may belong to a local network and a state network; they may also belong to a regional or national network.

Union catalogs, made available through networks, have made possible the "extended library." Individuals or libraries can use on-line terminals to identify a book, its location, and, in some cases, its availability.

The cost of an interlibrary loan, including the cost of telecommunication, is usually less than the cost of the material being borrowed. Computer equipment costs have either decreased or remained stable; staff and materials costs have risen. Networks flourished during the 1960s when the federal government began providing large sums of money of libraries, especially through the LSCA. During the 1970s, funding decreased, however, causing even closer cooperation. Improvements in telecommunications technology also spurred the growth of networks.

A special conference held in Virginia in 1970 on interlibrary communications and information networks recommended that a new National Commission on Libraries and Information Science be made a focal point for devising a national network of libraries and information centers. An important foundation for the effective sharing of information resources nationwide was established with the development of procedures and protocols for sharing authority records among the bibliographic utilities. These procedures and protocols will facilitate the uniform use the names and subject headings throughout the library community, not merely within individual collections. Libraries require networking links for two different aspects of their operation: They need links with other libraries and with bibliographic utilities to support their traditional processes, and they need links with the academic community to carry out their primary mission of providing students and scholars with access information.

Infrastructure

If we limit the consideration of networks to only those organizations using telecommunication devices, the formation and establishment of library networks has been prompted by four federal laws: (1) Library Services and Construction Act, Title III; (2) Higher

Education Act, Title II; (3) State Technical Services Act, and (4) Medical Library Assistance Act. Each of these laws may be called enabling legislation because funds are provided to develop networks to achieve some specific purpose outlined by the law. By accepting federal funds, the state agencies give precedence to federal laws over state laws. State rulings are adjusted to allow for the implementation of the federal law. Each state usually prepares a state plan, which must be reviewed and approved by the federal agency administering the program. Existing networks are quasi-official organizations with questionable legal identity and with powers resulting from a long series of contracts generally following this pattern and subject to legal interpretation of the following: (1) enabling federal law, (2) U.S. Bureau of Budget rules, (3) guidelines to the federal law, (4) state agency rules and the grant agreement between the federal and state agency, (5) state plans for that particular law, (6) the qualifying host institution's contract with the state agency (or federal agency), (7) the host institution regulations, and (8) the agreement between the network administrator and the host institution.

Duggan reviewed membership agreements or state contracts being used by 17 networks operating in one state. She found that no two networks had a similar instrument and that the lack of standardization was obvious even within the boundaries of one state. To avoid legal questions concerning sales tax for photocopy charges or other fees, liability for incomplete services to network users, and other matters, some networks call their contracts membership agreements. Formal written agreements of some type are considered essential in operating a successful network.

Legal questions may arise concerning who owns the databank used in a network, or from the procurement of an information bank by a network from a commercial agency, or even concerning a federal information bank. New academic institutions seeking accreditation by network access to collections can also present legal problems. Perhaps the most complex legal problems arise with network interfacing where incompatibility of operational policies, fee structures, users' access, funding base, and so forth become evident.

Any formula for network support requires consideration of cost elements, and these are embedded in the structural and operational decision of network construction. The questions of what kind of network, the projected stages of development, and who pays for what must be answered before a viable formula can be advanced; otherwise, we would be prescribing a fiscal remedy without benefit of diagnosis. Communication costs must be specified in terms of equipment, routing, channels, volumes, and outlets. S. Gilbert Prentiss, in describing the New York State Inter-Library Loan Network (NYSILL), suggested that a one-to-one charge from lender to borrower might be a simpler, less costly method of handling interlibrary loans than network membership fees or the passing of federal monies to the state agencies.

Types of Networks

Edward Walters has identified five forms of library networks: (1) the unit-cost networks, or bibliographic utilities-such as the Online Computer Library Center (OCLC) or the Research Libraries Information Network (RLIN) – with the size and revenue sources to raise capital for development; (2) the multistate regional auxiliary enterprise networks, such as AMIGOS (meaning friends) or the Southeastern Library Network (SOLINET), with their low capital investment and fee-based assessment and a more limited ability to amass capital; (3) the authority-sanctioned networks, such as ILLNET and FEDLINK (Federal Library Network), established by governments that have jurisdiction and draw on their authority to coerce the acceptance of standards and capital for new projects; (4) the discipline and type-of-library networks that are created for the purpose of sustaining either a discipline (law, medicine, or agriculture) or an institutional form (university or corporation); and (5) local consortia or proximity networks that are founded and sustained because geographical proximity makes library cooperation more timely and often more effective. These latter vary greatly in the kinds of organizations they include and in size, governance, and programs. A consortium is defined as a group formed through contractual arrange-ments. In 1934 a study of interinstitutional agreements indicated there were 113 such agreements.

Most consortia are established for special purposes. Members are allowed to resign when the group's purposes are no longer relevant. Most consortia ask for membership fees from the participating institutions, yet they are generally supported by federal money or a foundation grant. A distinct benefit of a consortium is the modest cost of participation for a much greater extension of resources and services.

Bibliographic Utilities

Four major bibliographic utilities serve North American libraries. They are know by the acronyms OCLC, RLIN, UTLAS, and WLN. Each has its own characteristics and special mission. For example, OCLC grew from a consortium (Ohio College Library Center) to support shared cataloging for libraries in Ohio into a worldwide organization with thousands of member libraries (Online Computer Library Center). UTLAS (University of Toronto Library Automation Center) began as a project to develop a union catalog for five new universities in Ontario, Canada. It evolved into a mission to support the Canadian library community in general, but it expanded to serve libraries and the United States and other countries. In 1985 it was sold to the International Thomson Organization and became a for-profit corporation. WLN began as the Washington Library Network and later became the Western Library Network. It is still a regional organization and provided a more limited range of services and products than does OCLS or UTLAS.

The libraries of the 1970s used the three large bibliographic utilities – WLN, OCLC, and RLIN. Though some were using COM, the local library catalog was primarily still a card catalog, with the cards being supplied by the utilities. The basic service of all three utilities was providing LC and member records for use in cataloging and to which holdings could be attached.

Online Computer Library Centre (OCLC)

The largest and most famous bibliographic utility was established in 1967 as the Ohio College Library Center to serve as a computerized regional processing center for libraries in Ohio. The goals of OCLS were (1) to support the member institutions by supplying information to them when and where they needed it, making it possible for them to cooperate in the educational and research activities of their individual users, and (2) to make the resources of all member libraries available to the faculty and students at each institution by means of an on-line union catalog. An off-line card production system was begun in 1970, followed by an on-line system for shared cataloging in 1971. The database consisted of

Library of Congress MARC records plus original cataloging contributed by participating libraries.

In 1973 OCLC offered membership to libraries outside Ohio, and the name was changed twice to reflect a larger outreach. During the 1980s OCLC began serving libraries in England and Japan.

OCLC's Union List Component supports the efforts of groups creating and maintaining national, state, and regional union lists of serials. Interlibrary loan participants can display these holdings through OCLS's interlibrary loan subsystem.

The interlibrary loan subsystem enhances communication. The electronic mailing of requests reduces turnaround time, and requests are sent to libraries known to hold the requested items. Studies have shown that the subsystem processes loan requests faster than TWX, the U.S. Postal Service, or package-delivery services.

Interlibrary loan requests are verified in the on-line union catalog, eliminating the need to search multiple sources to identify an item and find out who holds it and whether it can be borrowed. Bibliographic information from the on-line union catalog, as well as borrower and lender constant data, transfer automatically to an on-line ILL record, virtually eliminating the need for typing.

Up to five potential lenders per request may be chosen with the system forwarding the request to each potential lender, in turn, until it is filled. The status of the request can be checked at any time in the subsystem's electronic message file, which contains notices of new requests, recall and renewal notices, and other pertinent information. The system automatically notifies borrowers and lenders when items are overdue or lost. Policies and procedures for libraries and document suppliers can be obtained on-line in the name address directory.

OCLC offers lending credit for each item loaned through the OCLS interlibrary loan subsystem. The credit is recorded when the status of the record is changed to "shipped". Borrower and lender statistical reports can be ordered to keep up will ILL activity.

The Micro Enhancer software package helps save staff and terminal time by performing routine ILL record-keeping functions such as printing and batch updating ILL records. The Micro Enhancer software can be set to automatically dial up and log on to the OCLC on-line system, update ILL records entered off-line, and download and print ILL records. The updating functions that can be performed are shipping, receiving, returning, completing, canceling, recalling, and saying yes or no to "Pending," "Retry/Pend," and "Cond/Pend" requests, among other things.

The system is somewhat more cumbersome for the lender than for the borrower. The lender must enter a status response, return address, and shipping date in order not to lose a transaction from the file. With the addition of its EPIC on-line service, OCLC greatly expanded the search and retrieval capabilities of the OCLC database. Searching the OCLC database on EPIC provides subject access to the full database for the first time, in addition to allowing retrieval by many more access points. A growing number of document suppliers like the LC, National Agricultural Library, British Library Document Supply Center (BLDSC), and University Microfilms International are part of the OCLS's ILL network.

Research Libraries Information Network (RLIN)

The Research Libraries Group (RLG) was formed in 1974 to meet the needs of research libraries. In 1988 its membership consisted of 36 major U.S. universities and research institutions, each with a seat on the board of governors. After concluding that they needed to share a computer-based bibliographic processing system, RLG acquired BALLOTS (Bibliographic Automation of Large Library Operations Using a Time-Sharing System), the library automation system developed in the late 1960s and early 1970s for the Standard University libraries. BALLOTS was replaced in 1982 by a large application program known as the Integrated Technical Processing System (ITPS).

RLG operates an international computer network and a large mainframe computer system to provide the infrastructure for the RLIN. RLIN services, which include acquisitions, cataloging, and interlibrary loan, are provided by RLG members to institutions worldwide through the Cooperative Library Authority for Systems and Services (CLASS), based in San Jose, California.

Users can create and send loan requests through RLIN. Bibliographic information can be copied from an existing record to expedite the creation of requests. Borrowers can be notified that a request is being filled. Unfilled requests can be forwarded to another library. Users may check status of requests, renew, recall, send overdue notices, and collect statistics.

In addition to the RLG member library holdings, records are loaded into the database from the LC, CONSER (the CON version of SERials project), the National Library of Medicine, the Government Printing Office, and the British Library. Special databases in this network are the On-Line Avery Index to Architectural Periodicals, the Sale Catalog Index Project Input On-Line (SCIPIO), the Eighteenth Century Short Title Catalogue (ESTC), and the RLG Conspectus On-Line.

The On-Line Avery Index to Architectural Periodicals is produced and maintained by Columbia University. It indexes articles published since 1979 in over 1,000 journals in the fields of architecture, architectural design, history and practice of architecture, landscape architecture, city planning, historic preservation, and interior design and decoration. SCIPIO is a listing of art-sales catalogs.

The ESTC database contains bibliographic records for eighteenth-century publications from Great Britain and its colonies, as well as for English-language materials printed anywhere in the world during the same period. The British Library created the initial database, and the North American Center for ESTC, which is located at the University of California in Riverside, is adding North American holdings information as well as creating new bibliographic records for British imprints held by North American libraries. The American Antiquarian Society is also compiling American imprints in the North American Imprints Project.

Western Library Network (WLN)

The Western Library Network is the youngest and smallest of the on-line networks and began as the Washington Library Network. Several years of study preceded its development. It was established by state legislation in 1976 and began operations the following year. It was designed to serve the libraries of the state of Washington. Each library within the cooperative has the right to be represented in the development of goals, objectives, and day-to-day regulations, computer systems to support shared cataloging, retrospective conversion of catalog records to machine-readable form, and interlibrary lending. It is essentially a multitype library venture on a statewide basis that includes computer services, telecommunications services, interlibrary services, and reference and referral services.

WLN is subject to more governmental regulations than the other systems, because its headquarters is the Washington State Library. Its database is also smaller than those of the other systems. As a system, however; its quality is considered very high. The WLN software has been purchased by the University of Illinois at Urbana-Champaign and SOLINET, among others.

In the mid 1970s WLN introduced its on-line cataloging system and expanded to include the University of Alaska. It was one of the original participants in 1980 in the Linked Systems Project (LSP), a computer-to-computer linkage for the exchange of library information, which was to be used to create a national bibliographic network. It is, however, no longer a participant.

WLN, like RLG, provides on-line computer processing services to its members from the central offices. Others contract for the supply of network resources to their member libraries. Compared to other networks, WLN pricing is high.

University of Toronto Library Automation System (UTLAS)

UTLAS began as a project to develop a union catalog for five new universities in Ontario, Canada, developed into the University of Toronto Library Automation System to support libraries in Canada, and then expanded to serve libraries in other parts of the world. In 1985 UTLAS was sold to the International Thomson Organization and became a for-profit corporation.

The University of Toronto updated its microform catalog by use of the UTLAS system. The university began converting its catalog records to machine-readable form in 1959. Shortly thereafter efforts to form consortia among Ontario libraries were initiated. UTLAS network organization efforts paralleled system development efforts. It is now used in hundreds of libraries across Canada. By the mid-1970s UTLAS had a large on-line technical processing support system in operation. In 1980 Rochester Institute of Technology became the first library in the United States to use UTLAS.

Each user of UTLAS owns its own database and may decide whether to charge other libraries a royalty for using its records. Annual costs are, therefore, unpredictable, and the costs of specific products and services are unstable.

The major database resources are available through UTLAS-MARC, CAN-MARC, BNB (British National Bibliography) and others. From the on-line database other resources, including microform and book catalogs, are made available. The now-commercial UTLAS has a copyright on its database but makes it available to nonmember institutions.

Types of Local Network

Regional Networks arose from library consortia, taking advantage of available technology and technical expertise. The regional networks made major contributions by developing approaches to the organization, governance, and financing of decentralized cooperative efforts.

Regional or multistate networks are usually privately funded by their own members. The political constraints and geographical boundaries of a statewide network do not apply. Examples of such networks are AMIGOS, which serves the Southwest; CAPCON (Capital Consortium), which serves libraries in the Washington, D.C. area; NELINET (New England Library Information Network); OHIONET; PALINET (Pennsylvania Area Library Network), which serves libraries in Pennsylvania, Delaware, Maryland, and New Jersey; SOLINET; and others. Federal libraries scattered all over the country have their own network called FEDLINK.

These brokers serve as liaisons between member libraries and OCLC, contracting for OCLC services on a time-sharing basis. They assist with OCLC installation, provide operators' manuals and newsletters, conduct training sessions, and collect fees for OCLC usage.

Midwest Region Library Network (MIDLNET)

The Midwest Region Library Network (MIDLNET) was established to solve the resource-sharing problems of four net lenders-the University of Illinois at Urbana, the Illinois State Library, the Minnesota Interlibrary Telecommuni-cations Exchange (MINITEX), and the Wisconsin Interlibrary Loan Service (WILS). The libraries placing requests through MIDLNET experience the advantages of comprehensiveness, speed, and reliability not available to institutions borrowing and lending independently.

Pennsylvania Area Library Network (PALINET)

PALINET, with offices in Philadelphia, is an outgrowth of the Union Library Catalogue of Pennsylvania. The catalog was microfilmed and sold to major libraries in the area when the OCLC database was made available. Many of the member libraries began using the OCLC database. PALINET.

PALINET is not the perfect answer to interlibrary loan, however. The associate director of the network, Dorothy Russell, indicated in early 1982 that there were five major factors working against perfect interlibrary loan in the PALINET region: (1) not all libraries belong to the same bibliographic network-most belong to OCLC, but some belong to RLIN; (2) not all libraries choose the same form of transmission for ILL requests (OCLC, TWX, mail or telephone); (3) the multistate and multiinterest nature of the network means that interlibrary loan is not as controllable and definable as it is in some single-state networks. Interlibrary loan codes abound; (4) PALINET lacks a comprehensive and unified delivery service; and (5) funding problems.

Multitype Area Networks

Networking and *multitype library cooperation* are not synonymous terms. Multitype library cooperation is defined as the cooperation of two or more legal library entities in sharing resources, personnel, facilities, and/or programs with a library or libraries of other types and having different legal bases. A multitype library network is a cooperative structure that crosses jurisdictional, and often political, boundaries to join several types of libraries (academic, school, special, and public) in a common enterprise. The multitype library *network* is usually an interface between two more or less highly articulated single-type library cooperatives. In many areas of the country, the definitions of these two multitype functions are not so precise and blend into one.

Publicly funded networks, usually statewide, are often supported with LSCA funds through a state library agency. Some doubt is expressed that these diverse institutions can really share services. There was also concern that enabling legislation and tax support, or hard money, is not as easily obtained as the soft start-up money received from the federal government through LSCA. The statewide networks, such as the Indiana Cooperative Library Services Authority (InCOLSA), MINITEX, and ILLINET, are multitype.

The study showed that the involvement of 243 schools increased ILL requests by only 3.6 percent in 1981 and 3.7 percent in 1982. It confirmed the belief that different types of libraries satisfy requests among themselves rather than going to other types of libraries.

The addition of the schools, however, did bring 116 unique periodical titles into the network's resources. None of the titles in this particular study attracted requests, so they were only a *potential* resource that did not change supply.

The effects of LSCA funding on the development of multitype cooperatives are far-reaching. LSCA requires that funds be administered through state agencies and that these agencies produce long-range plans, coordinating agency programs with library programs in colleges and schools and other public and private institutions offering library services.

A statewide network can be a single-function (for example, interlibrary loan) or a multifunction network. Many types of governance structures are possible. Many complex legal, technical, and philosophical issues are involved.

In contrast to the informal union list type of cooperative, multitype library networks that provide ILL service are usually formal in structure. They have a paid staff, continuous funding by state and federal appropriations, and perhaps membership fees, and they usually compensate resource libraries. There are many examples of such statewide, single-function, multitype library cooperatives. Among them are NYSILL; ILLINET; TIE (the Texas Informa-tion Exchange); and FLIN (Florida Library Information Network).

Several studies have concentrated on multitype networks within a state or region. Van House pointed out that school and special libraries have different priorities than do public and academic libraries and they are more constrained by their parent organizations. Libraries involve themselves in multitype networks to reach their own objectives, even though they differ widely in political sophistication and financial backing. It is necessary to know the environment in which each type of library operates and what is objectives are to know what the advantages of participating in a multitype might be. Libraries entering networks should be analyzed to determine their constraints, their support systems, their social and economic back-grounds, their services, their expertise, their resources, and their expectations. Such preparation will assist multitype originators in creating networks responsive to situational needs instead of creating networks defined by what convention says they should be.

There appear to be three primary approaches to network building. One approach has the primary focus of activity at the state library agency, another has the activity focus at academic libraries, and the last uses a nonprofit corporation with a relationship to the state library. Concerning state networks, there are questions that arise regarding enabling legislation, relationships among libraries of various types and sizes, funding, organization and administration, and relationships with vendors. To be more specific, one of the first questions that must be answered is whether the state library will play a major role. These agency heads are often public library oriented and they may even be politically motivated. Political problems, including funding and governance, are more difficult to overcome than are technical problems.

States having regional, multitype library systems may be more likely to develop statewide networks because the fear of losing control has already been addressed. The all-important question then becomes, "Will state governments assume the responsibility for funding statewide library networks"? LSCA funds are also obtained through grant proposals written by the state library.

What happens if large libraries do or do not participate in state networks? Some have not, thinking they would become net lenders, increasing surprised to learn that the pooled resources of the smaller libraries met the needs, for the most part, of the patrons of the smaller libraries, and they were not called upon as often as they had anticipated. They also reaped some benefits of being able to borrow from smaller, specialized libraries. There is some indication, however, that all librarians involved have not acquired the spirit of the true multitype network.

Major Owens was right when he predicted in an article in the *Library Journal* in 1976 that local and city powers would diminish and state powers would increase. He further predicted the importance of multitype networks, expressing a need for a state agency to act as coordinator. This approach to state-based networking has been adopted by many states. Leadership in automation and networking has been provided by Illinois, New York, California, Colorado, and Indiana.

New York State Interlibrary Loan Network (NYSILL)

NYSILL, begun in 1967, assigns to the state library the responsibility for switching and screening messages. Public library systems and other consortia (SUNY biomedical network, FAUL, [Five Associated University Libraries], METRO, and others), as well as academic libraries, were expected to fill as many requests within their own jurisdictions as possible. Participation grants were provided to referral libraries, as well as reimbursement of costs for each transaction to subject resource libraries. School libraries were not included because age limit was restricted to 18. Other libraries were arranged in hierarchical tiers. Each referral library had a TWX installed to speed communications.

Several revisions to the system were made, including allowing large academic institutions to borrow from one another without going through NYSILL, thus speeding up service. Copies of the requests had to be sent to the state library to ensure reimbursement. The system was at first, however, time-consuming and costly, with only 55 percent of requests being filled. Average cost per request filled was $15.80.

Further refinement of the system resulted in improve-ment in the four factors by which system performance may be measured-volume, filling rates, elapsed time, and decrease in costs. Local delivery systems and first class mail for photocopies improved delivery.

Nelson Associates conducted a survey of borrowing among the multitype libraries in the state in order to assess NYSILL's contributions to overall interlibrary loan in the state. Forty-four separate findings were reported in this very detailed study. Of the 16 recommendations, the first was that NYSILL should be funded as an ongoing system, not as an experimental program. Other recommendations were that more administrative and planning help should be obtained from the state library, the teletype format should be revised, interfacing with other systems in the state should be studied, automation of record keeping should be implemented, and an analysis should be made of requests not filled. The final recommendation advised the state library to delay plans for a proposed delivery system until the volume of interlibrary loans increased.

Illinois Library and Information Network (ILLINET)

The network was evaluated in 1974 to identify problems, to make recommendations for solutions to the problems, and to develop a model for continuous evaluation of the network. Information was sought about the requests as well as about the handling of the requests. Member libraries were stratified by type, and a random sample was drawn from each type.

Over two-thirds of all requests during February 1975 were for adults. Almost twenty-five percent were for college students; 8 percent were for high school students; and 2 percent were for elementary school students. Eighty-four percent of the requests analyzed were for authors and titles. Eleven percent were information requests, most of them going to system-headquarters libraries.

Requests were further analyzed by type and subject, by type of library submitting requests, and by other criteria. One of the findings was that almost two-thirds of the public library serial requests were for items published in the previous five years. Half of the public library monograph requests were for books published in the previous five years.

Floria Library Information Network (FLIN)

Florida has a statewide network with the Bureau of Interlibrary Cooperation established at the Florida State Library and a network advisory committee to coordinate activities. Clusters of libraries also work together within the state to form consortia. One example is the Southeast Florida Library Information Network (SEFLIN). It includes populous Broward County and nearby areas and provides document delivery services.

FLIN public on-line libraries use protocol tiers to prevent any library from becoming overburdened and to distribute the work load equitably. Local reciprocal and other agreements for resource sharing take precedence over FLIN protocols. For example, members of SEFLIN will exhaust its resources before going to FLIN and following FLIN protocols. These local agreements make up the first protocol tier. The State Library of Florida is the second tier; the third tier is composed of regional resource centers (Large public libraries); the fourth tier is composed of public library systems and school libraries; the fifth tier is composed of non-ARL academic libraries; the sixth tier is composed of ARL libraries; and the last tier is special libraries.

A different set of tiers is used for academic libraries, with the second and third tier being composed of those libraries, and the state library being moved to the fourth tier. There is also some shifting in the other tiers. Similarly, the community college libraries, the private academic libraries, and special libraries have their own set or rearranged protocols, allowing types of libraries to borrow from each other as much as possible.

During the July 1991 to June 1992 time period, 190,008 items were supplied through FLIN for requests submitted through OCLC, U.S. mail, and courier. This figure represents an increase of 20,078 items (12 percent) over the number of items supplied from July 1990 to June 1991. Improved networking and regional library consortia are two reasons resource-sharing figures continue to rise in Florida.

Books were 67.9 percent of the items supplied, and 32.1 percent were photocopies. The State Library of Florida supplied 19.1 percent of the total. It not only supplies material from its own collection but also refers requests for FLIN libraries that are not on-line to OCLC. Other items were supplied by multitype libraries as follows: (1) regional resource center libraries, 20.4 percent; (2) Florida State University (working under a grant with the state library), 9.6 percent; (3) other state university system libraries, 24.8 percent; (4) private academic libraries, 11.7 percent; (5) public libraries, 7.3 percent; (6) community college, 3.9 percent; and (7) special libraries, 2.5 percent. A new group called Selective User Libraries supplied 0.8 percent.

Other Role of Network

Automation has precipitated large-scale development of statewide networks, many of them evolving from a TWX or other system. Some states have found automation provided through bibliographic utilities too expensive and thus have worked to develop an individualized system. In Connecticut the five largest public libraries were, in the beginning of the state network, on a teleprinter circuit joined to the state library. The network was reinforced by United Parcel delivery, in addition to mail service. Like many other statewide networks during the 1960s, the state library also maintained a TWX system to exchange bibliographic information. At first it exchanged with Rhode Island. The TWX exchange was further expanded by the state universities of New England through NELINET.

The KIC (Kansas Information Circuit) Interlibrary Loan Network, has proved to be a low-cost alternative to OCLC's interlibrary loan subsystem, and by maintaining most of OCLC's features, it has become the preferred transmission method for in-state requests by even those libraries with OCLC capability. For those libraries in Kansas that exclusively used ALA forms or the old Texas Instruments network, KIC has been hailed as the most significant resource-sharing advance since the COM union catalog was introduced in 1977. It did not come easy, however. The amount of effort required to bring each library on-line and to maintain the network was horrendous, according to the system administrator.

Massachusetts' first formal automation plan was approved by the board of library commissioners in 1983. Fifteent million dollars in state and federal funds were allocated to automated resource sharing in Massachusetts. Funding was used for system planning, for central site hardware and software for 12 circulation and ILL systems, for telecommunications plans and equipment, for expansion of dial-up access micros, and for union lists of serials.

Five Associated University Libraries (FAUL)

FAUL is an example of a network that was not really a network in its own right, so it did not survive. It was a consortium dependent on NYSILL, national ILL codes, TWX, telephone, United Parcel Service (UPS), the U.S. Post Office, and the like.

FAUL adopted its constitution in 1967. It was composed of the libraries of the five largest universities in upstate New York: SUNY-Binghamton, SUNY-Buffalo, Cornell, Syracuse, and the University of Rochester.

There were four primary reasons for the formation of consortium: (1) the rapid growth of SUNY and the New York State Library; (2) the bandwagon growth of library consortia; (3) the promise of federal and private funding of library consortia; and (4) a belief by the chief librarians that the problems of academic research libraries are unique insofar as libraries go but are fairly similar among themselves. Shared resources was only one of the services expected to be derived from this cooperative arrangement.

Financial support was provided by member libraries. Their dues ($13,000 in 1970) provided central office staff salaries, travel, equipment, space rental, consultants, and small research and development projects. FAUL was intelligible for New York State funds, because it was not incorporated.

Single-Type Networks

Many networks began as single-type networks designed to foster cooperation and communication among libraries serving the same general purpose. Public libraries within a state or region, because they are funded with public money and because they serve the same type of clientele, have cooperated for a long period of time.

Groups of research libraries have also created single-type networks. Research libraries, like public libraries, have common goals with a very specific group of borrowers to serve. Two examples of this type of network are the Association of Research Libraries (ARL) and the Center for Research Libraries (CRL).

Single-type networks predominated until expensive computer systems began to be used. OCLC, especially, caused single-type networks to gradually become multitype.

The National Library of Medicine coordinates a national biomedical library network called DOCLINE, which provides document delivery and supports an automated document routing and referral system DOCLINE, which was implemented in 1985, is similar in operation to the OCLC ILL subsystem. Users may create and receive requests, monitor request status, update requests, receive messages, and receive statistical reports.

Before DOCLINE was implemented the Regional Medical Library Network handled millions of requests in the traditional way. By building on an already existing network, DOCLINE developers could concentrate on technical problems and avoid many of the organizational and policy issues associated with network development.

Local Area Networks (LAN)

In the 1980s the microcomputer became widely available, and the librarian's dream of having an integrated on-line system began to seem possible, even for smaller libraries. The problem with creating local on-line systems is that we are still tied to the bibliographic utilities. Martin believes that we must measure the level at which we can afford to be "good citizens," contributing standard data to nationwide database.

The idea for local cooperation among health sciences libraries in St. Louis originated from the databases and technology that had existed in the area since 1962 the Washington University PHILSOM system (Periodical Holdings in Libraries of Schools of Medicine)-which included the machine-readable holdings records of most St. Louis health-related libraries. The network was provided by OCTANET, a regional ILL system developed by Washington University and administered by the Midcontinental Regional Medical Library Program.

OCTANET was the prototype for DOCLINE, the National Library of Medicine's ILL system. When DOCLINE became available in 1987, OCTANET was discontinued. Holdings of the smaller health sciences libraries in the region were not yet in DOCLINE, however, and the St. Louis medical librarians consortium was reluctant to give up electronic access to local collections.

Washington University responded positively to their requests for a local network, on several conditions. The consortium would have to guarantee financial support, and the system would have to pay for itself. It would also operate on a trial basis, during which time members would determine if a local system, in addition to DOCLINE, was needed.

In the beginning, PHILNET's primary purpose was shared document delivery. Its success encouraged network members to expand its capabilities beyond interlibrary loan. By 1983, Washington University's Bibliographic Access and Control System (BACS) was available to offices, laboratories, and other remote locations through a hard-wire network and dial-in access. Through the BACS consortium, serials control, cataloging, on-line public access catalog, circulation, management reports, E-mail, and access to bibliographic databases are now available in addition to automated interlibrary loan. BACS and PHILNET demonstrated that, by using technology and databases already in place, local libraries can benefit by working together within large networks.

Since the early 1980s, librarians have shifted from total cooperation to strong support of local systems. There are several reasons for this. (1) microcomputers make it possible for libraries to accomplish locally what once could be achieved only by cooperating with others; (2) Librarians have discovered that the autonomy of a local system is often preferable to the requirement of operating in a specified manner according to network procedures; and (3) the private sector has discovered the library market to be profitable and is offering services bibliographic utilities will no longer be needed, but rather that they will need to continue.

What used to be done on a TWX machine can be done using a microcomputer. Interlibrary loan networking went from the TWX machine to participation in bibliographic utilities using mainframe databases. Now the whole thing is being localized using microcomputers and communications networks. LANS (Local Area Networks) are being used to connect personal computers. The networks are an attempt to provide resource-sharing capabilities to the end user who has access to a personal computer. Individual patrons may access the library catalog from their home terminals. It requires the addition of modems and ports to the computers and appropriate software.

Brigham Young University's Law School and Law Library has gained national recognition for its own local, integrated computing facilities, which are linked to other campus facilities to form a local area network. The University of Delaware has expanded its computerized library system to offer statewide toll-free access to the on-line system on the Newark campus. Individuals throughout the state can now dial from home computers to search through the system's bibliographic records. A particular item can be requested at no charge through regular ILL procedures at a local public library.

Interlibrary loan has been speeded up by widespread participation in bibliographic utilities available through remote mainframe databases. The whole system can be localized using microcomputers and communications networks. Interfaces can save personnel time by transferring and reformatting MARC records from a bibliographic utility into a local database. Accuracy can be increased by eliminating rekeying, and records can be made available instantly.

Interfaces used with the NOTIS (Northwestern University) software allow users in several statewide systems to access public catalogs of large university libraries in their state. Users in Indiana public, school, and special libraries access the catalogs of eight Indiana research libraries using SULAN/LINKWAY, a point-and-click user interface to the NOTIS on-line catalog. SULAN is an acronym for the State University Library Automation Network, and LINKWAY is an IBM hypermedia software product. SULAN/LINKWAY intercepts NOTIS screens, processes them, and redisplays them using color graphics. The increased visibility of research library collections increases the demand for the items in those collections. SULAN/LINKWAY will also form the platform for many new services such as expert systems and links to other types of data.

Microcomputers have led to more widespread cooperation in foreign libraries, as well. Italian libraries, for example, had very little cooperation because of a lack of funding. In 1985 two public libraries near Florence automated their services using microcomputers. Data are exchanged using floppy disks, thereby creating a Floppy Disk Local Area Network, or FLAN. The software program TINlib, which is based on the database TINman, was translated and adapted to the needs of Italian libraries.

Each library runs the same copy of the program on two separate databases - its own catalog and the data relative to the latest acquisitions onto a floppy disk and sends it to the project coordinating office. The data are loaded into the union catalog from the disk using TINlib's import procedure. Thus gradually the participating libraries' union catalog is being constructed.

Every month the union catalog data contained on a tape cassette are sent to the libraries where, using a tape streamer, operators load it in a few minutes into the second database present in TINlib. As a collective catalog is updated only by the coordinating office, each copy sent to the libraries completely supersedes the previous one.

This catalog is consulted in the same way as is the library's own local catalog.

A National Network

In the mid-1970s, most people saw the need for a national network with the major players consisting of large research libraries such as the LC, bibliographic centers such as WLN and OCLC, the regional networks such as SOLINET and NELINET, and private-sector suppliers of library services. Gordon Williams, director of the CRL in Chicago, believed that a single dedicated ILL center, providing fast access to all libraries and providing access as a right rather than as a privilege, would greatly improve ILL access. It is not certain, he said, whether one or more centers are needed or where they should be located. He suggested that until more information was made available, it would be best for the United States to copy the British Library Lending Division model, even though our greater population and greater landmass might present some problems.

After a thorough study of interlibrary loan problems in all types of libraries, Rolland Stevens concluded that a periodicals lending center along the lines of the British Library Lending Division (Boston Spa) is not the total solution to our lending problems. The differences in geography and library resources between the United States and Great Britain argue against the success and the need for such a center in this country. Our money and efforts, according to Stevens, would be better spent on improving bibliographic and local information and on building a hierarchical lending system based on present library resources.

To build a national network it will be necessary to standardize the policies and procedures, including prices, of libraries involved in the network. Despite the interlibrary loan code, there are almost as many policies and prices as there are libraries. It will be impossible to ask the government to subsidize a network with all sorts of variant rules.

John Berry made an interesting point when he said that it is difficult to refute the argument that the first priority of academic research libraries is to libraries, few, if any, exist without direct aid from government in one form or another. Not one of them pays local, state, or federal taxes. Gifts to money and materials are tax deductible.

Lower postal rates and copyright protection are also provided to libraries through the government.

The LC database, called LOCIS (Library of Congress Information System) is subdivided into two segments called SCORPIO (Subject-content-Oriented Retriever for Processing Information Online) and MUMS (Multiple Use MARC System). SCORPIO contains books, citations for selected periodical articles and U.S. government publications since 1976, federal legislation since 1973, copyright registrations since 1978, and referral information on organizations. MUMS contains (1) books cataloged, books being cataloged, Books on order, and some books located in other libraries; (2) and owned by LC or selected other research libraries; (3) maps cataloged and owned by the LC and some cataloged by other libraries; (4) recorded sound materials and music scores; (5) visual materials; (6) files with records for several types of items, such as manuscripts, NUC holdings, in-process material at the LC; and (7) records with authorized name and subject headings, and cross-references, used for LC cataloging.

LOCIS was called a powerful cataloging tool, and the authors indicated that they had been able to provide public services that were unavailable before having access to LOCIS. The ILL unit at the University of Kentucky used SCORPIO and MUMS for title verification and for electronic transmission of requests. Users in the unit concluded that for libraries not already using an electronic method of transmission such as OCLC or RLIN for obtaining materials, the LC on-line system of transmission (FETCH) would be worthwhile in expediting ILL requests. Their experience suggested that for a large research library, processing ILL requests via a bibliographic utility-OCLC or RLIN-seems to be the best solution.

In reviewing 20 years of national library network development in 1985, Barbara Markuson noted, "The reality is that our tremendous system of nationwide access to library holdings would stop dead in its tracks without constant local commitment and financial support." Because the libraries that participated in large-scale cooperative or automation efforts were large institutions geographically dispersed across the country, a national network seemed the most likely way to interconnect them. As the number of libraries involved in automation increased, small and decentralized clusters of libraries were needed. Regional service units were soon developed to meet the need.

Continued growth in library automation fueled by the availability of micro-and mini-computer-based turnkey systems and by the large number of bibliographic records and holdings data in standard formats has brought the current interests in further decentralization from national networks-or centralization at the state level.

Connecting Networks

Although the LC would seem to be the appropriate source for a nationwide network, as has been suggested many times, its primary influence has been with the development of the MARC record and the activity of the Network Advisory Committee (NAC). In 1976 the LC set up a special office to investigate how it could facilitate networking and perhaps derive benefits for itself. The office organized the NAC as a major planning tool. The LC Network Development Office, the NAC and the NAC-sponsored Network Technical Architecture Group focused on two networking components that set the stage for Linked Systems Project. The Network Advisory Group was formed from representatives of several ongoing systems to help the LC in coordination of the components of this evolving national system. The group, which met for the first time in February 1977, consisted of representatives from the ALA, AMIGOS, the ARL, BALLOTS, the Bibliographic Center for Research, the California Library Authority for Systems and Service, the Council for Computerized Library Networks, the Council on Library Resources, the Federal Library Committee, the LC; MIDLNET, NCLIS, National Library of Medicine, NELINET, OCLC, RLG, the Southeastern Library Network, the University of Chicago, WLN, and the Western Interstate Library Coordinating Organization.

The primary focus of the group was to search for a way to enable cost-effective system-to-system communication that would facilitate sharing of the large resources of records building up at the three bibliographic utilities-WLN, OCLC, and RLIN. This could make the U.S. network configuration respond like a single system while retaining the advantages of a distributed (three-site) system.

The second major focus was on sharing authority records. Studies in these two areas of emphasis were carried out. An ad hoc computer-to-computer link was set up between the LC and the RLG computer system. Protocol specification work for linking computers was supported by NCLIS, and a program for sharing authority records was organized by the LC.

When libraries began to put their records into the bibliographic utilities the situation began to change. This was largely because the utilities are basically competing organizations.

There are three major areas where standardization is needed as libraries move into the linked OPAC environment: data, communications, and user interface. Care needs to be taken to ensure that standards are specified in all system procurements.

Much planning experimenting, coordinating, learning, and implementing has gone into the LSP. In the early years, standards were not ready, but they were starting to appear when implementation began. The first part of a fully linked system was operating in early 1985.

Networks Planning

For a library just beginning to investigate the possibilities of networking, choices are available among systems with a long survival record. Because the networks are changing constantly, however, a library should not make a decision on a network by copying another library's decision unless it was a very recent one and the libraries are very similar in nature.

As more libraries are becoming involved in networks, network systems and organizations are viewed as vendors vying for the library's business rather than as partners. Librarians, therefore, are joining networks by singing contracts for specific services. If another vendor should offer better services at less cost, the library may change networks or vendors.

A combination of start-up expenses, fixed ongoing costs incurred regardless of a library's volume of cataloging activity, and variable costs that depend on the amount and nature of services used are incurred by libraries using bibliographic utilities. In the case of OCLC, for example, required start-up expenditures include those for workstations and their installation, site preparation, establishing the library's catalog card profile, and staff training. Examples of fixed ongoing costs include the cost of leased telephone lines, ongoing training, printed operators' manuals and other documentation, and network membership fees if the subscriber joins OCLC through a regional network. A telecommunication system normally can be analyzed in terms of the costs and performance of three major hardware components: (1) user terminals, (2) communication lines, and (3) the central computer and data storage system. In addition, a substantial cost in most systems is associated with the software that enables the user to operate the system simply and efficiently. Maintenance and operating costs either can be associated with each of these subsystems of lumped as a single separate item.

OCLC has a larger database, a broader financial base, and a more sophisticated ILL subsystem and regional structure. Twenty regional networks offer OCLC services. Until recently, one of the chief disadvantages of OCLC was its limited search capabilities. It has also criticized for its inability to perform as a local on-line catalog and its lack of interest in cooperation among the networks.

Its powerful searching capability, higher quality of records, and ability to serve as a local on-line catalog are the features that have caused RLIN to be praised as the system of the future, even though OCLC has the advantage presently. RLIN is disadvantaged by a smaller database, slower growth, and a more expensive system. It has promoted network cooperation and unrestricted access to its database.

It was announced on July 10, 1991, in the *Chronicle of Higher Education* that the RLG rejected a proposal to connect its national electronic network with that of the OCLC. The connection would have cut costs and reduced duplication of library materials. Under the proposal, members of both organizations would have had access to the computer databases of the other while continuing to maintain their own networks. Although admitting that the link is a vision long held by the library community, RLG president James Michalko said that his consortium objected to the basic features of the link as proposed, its administration, and the timetable for establishing it. OCLC would not commit to link the networks before 1994, but RLG wanted the connection established sooner. Representatives of both groups held out the possibility that they may yet reach an agreement.

To help librarians in choosing a network, Rouse and Rouse prepared an analysis aimed at providing a methodology for answering questions of performance and cost. Using ILLINET as an example, the consultants presented a procedure for quantitative assessment of the impact of computer technologies and their various combinations on ILL activities.

It is quite another matter to begin a new network. The first stage of network implementation is planning. When agreement is reached on goals, network planners must win support for their program from librarians, trustees, education officials, members of the state executive department, and the state legislature. It must be decided to select the legislation rather than the appropriation route to achieve network funding goals. The legislation route will be preferred for continuity of state funding through a legislated formula. The appropriation route may ensure an earlier start of the network.

If the legislation route is selected, planners must be as precise as possible in drafting the bill, including such information as the purpose of the program, its administration at the state level, the types of network organizations eligible for state aid, the standards for eligibility of networks, and state-aid formula factors. Of key importance to state officials will be the maximum state cost of the formula and the appropriation level for the first year of operation. The network legislative bill must then be explained to and understood by those in state government who make the decisions on all "money bills." The bill must be approved by the legislature and the governor.

2

ON-LINE NETWORK MEANING & SCOPE

The Dynamics of Information

We are living in the so-called 'Information Age'. Information is a vast, dynamic and inexhaustible resource that affects all disciplines and all people. Information is used to support education, research and development and the production of goods and services for the community, all of which go to improve the quality of life. Information by itself has no value. Its value comes from its communication and use. Communication involves the transfer of information from one person to the other and is affected by the variables of time and space. The most effective communication is interactive and takes place at the same time and in the same place, such as personal communication between colleagues in a conference or a meeting. However, the process of communicating information is rendered difficult due to several inherent problems as under:

1. The existence and continuing growth of information due to the so-called 'information explosion' and 'information overload':
2. The interdisciplinary nature of information;
3. Information scatter in numerous sources;
4. Geographical, language and other barriers to communication.

The Impact of Technology in Information Handling

In order to overcome these barriers, there exists today a vast array of electronic tools and techniques for accumulating, storing, organizing, retrieving, communi-cating and interpreting information on a world-wide scale in a volume and at a speed and with an accuracy that would have been impossible hardly a few years ago.

We are experiencing now what might be called 'the push of technology' and its impact on every facet of information handling. The advent of the digital computer and the advances in the telecommunication and audio-visual technologies have opened up new possibilities in dealing with the problems arising from the collection, organization and dissemination of a vast amount of information.

While the spectacular growth of the computer and communication technology in the last few decades is notable, what is even more notable is the rapid way these technologies are merging. The computer and communi-cation technologies are not only merging but are also converging with related technologies such as printing and photography. When all these elements are fully integrated, the resultant capability for information transfer and exchange could create a form of material information interdependence and the development of a totally new information infrastructure for society.

Computerize Databases

For decades, libraries and documentation centres had become accustomed to the fact that the 'currency' of most abstracting and indexing services, i.e., the time-lapse between the publication of a paper in a primary journal and its subsequent coverage in abstracting/indexing sources, was of the order of six months of more. The cost of printing and distribution of abstracting/indexing journals was also increasing rapidly. Because of these reasons, the secondary publishers turned to the computer to assist them in the preparation of their publications and so arrest the delays and spiralling costs of production. The relative cost of processing and storage of data using the modern computer facilities was declining since the seventies and new more efficient software was available.

The most important byproduct of this change was in the method of preparation of abstracting and indexing services by keeping the text on magnetic media capable of being processed, in general, by a computer. The primary purpose was to use this form of material to 'drive' typesetting equipment for the production of the printed volumes. During the process, the machine readable records become the most useful byproducts as databases, enabling the users to get access to the required information at a faster rate. In the beginning, the databases were simply based on using the computer to sort the data into categories or select material in a given area. This type of service was normally provided in batch mode, that is, the data was loaded into a computer and compared with a 'query' which selected the items. The output was a subset of the data, which covered the subject of the 'query'. Further progress in data processing has made it possible to carry out this procedure in 'real time', that is, by continuous interaction with the data to refine the 'query' based on previous results. This development has been brought about by the use of direct-access computer memories, file inversion techniques, sophisticated retrieval software, by means of which possible combination in search logic could be tested during the search operation itself.' These systems require that the computer be interrogated by a terminal on which the successive trial stages of search could be 'played back' by the computer to the user in 'real time'. The display either on a video screen or the terminal printer of actual references retrieved with complete bibliographic data would suggest to the user further possibilities to be investigated during the search.

Online Systems and Services

The term 'online' now embodies many concepts. Literally, it means that the user is in contact with the computer through some direct linkage. In practice, it implies very much more and now is accepted as being some kind of individual terminal attached to the computer either by a direct line or over the telephone network.

The key technological components of online systems are computers that can operate in time-shared mode and teleprocessing with terminal equipment. Additional capabilities that make this an effective alternative are large amount of low-cost random access storage and an extensive and low-cost data communication systems.

These requirements are satisfied today and have resulted in rapid development of online services. The computers operate with control programs that

1. interface with many communication lines;
2. interpret and execute search formulations and commands interactively with the user;
3. format, sequence and transmit the related output records;
4. do this for many users simultaneously while keeping detailed accounting records of these activities; and
5. operate concurrently with some background jobs, such as, file conversion, statistical analysis and new programme development work.

Large amounts of random access memory are used today in the major online systems. Online strorage capacity is needed primarily for

1. the basic operating systems and search service programs;
2. storage of intermediate results from searches (over one million characters per user are provided in some systems);
3. storage of master files;
4. storage of inverted indexes of the files (often two to three times the storage requirements of the files themselves).

Extensive communications capability must exist in any online service that is designed to accommodate a diversity of users. Usually, national and international databases can be accessed by one or more of the communication media-the telex network or the automatic telephone network or a specialized (dedicated) data network. In broad terms, the capacity, speed and error rate improve as one moves from telex through telephone links to a specialized data network. Each of these networks is or may be connected to other similar networks in other countries and, therefore, offer the possibilities for international access to information services. The optimum solution is provided by the availability of a specialized data network which, when used in conjunction with the public telephone network for 'local' access, offers the most reliable and economic means for access to databases. It should be pointed out that all databases access services support telex connections and that the reliability on international (direct dialing) telephone circuits is not always very good.

An organization wishing to have access to databases should be equipped with a terminal which can very widely as a result of the economic resources of the organization concerned and of the nature of service proposed. The following example of possible configurations range from the simplest to the most sophisticated-telex terminal, teleprinter, teleprinter with built-in acoustic coupler, visual display unit with printer, and microcomputer. The types of terminal and transit network which may serve for given speeds of data transmission are given on the next page.

In order that the various terminals (except telex) can be used for access via telephone circuits, it will be necessary to use a modem (modulator-demodulator) which is a device to convert the digital signals coming from the terminal into a form suitable for transmission on the (analogue) telephone network. However, terminals are now available with modem built in.

Online Networks

The terms 'networks' can be used in different ways. Loosely defined, it can refer to any kind of formal cooperative arrangement where people agree to exchange information or resources. Many of the library networks in existence today are largely based on exchange arrangements. The kind of networking, which is referred to here, however, is electronic networking that permits sharing and remote use of hardware, software and databases. Computer readable databases now exist in large numbers. It is estimated that more than 600 such databases containing over 100 million records are available now for online search and retrieval through networks.

Transmission Speed in Baud	No. of Characters/ Second	Transit Network	Type of Terminal
50 Baud	50/Characters/Second	Telex network	Telex
110 to 300 baud	10 to 30 characters/ second	Automatic telephone network/ Specialized network	Visual Display Unit terminal + Printer or tele-printer or Micro computer
1200 baud	120 Characters/ second	Automatic telephone network or specialized data network	VDU Terminal + Printer, Teleprinter, Microcomputer

(Contd.)

Transmission Speed in Baud	No. of Characters/ Second	Transit Netwofk	Type of Terminal
Higher speeds 2400, 4800 and 9600 bauds	240, 480, 960 characters/second	Specialised data network or dedicated line point to point	VDU terminal + Printer; Micro-computer

NB:

1. One baud is equivalent in general to one bit (or basic unit of of information) per second.
2. In telex a character five bits long is employed while in other methods a character of 8 bits is generally used when two or three control bits per character are accounted for it is a good approximation to calculate teh character rate by dividing the baud rate by ten.

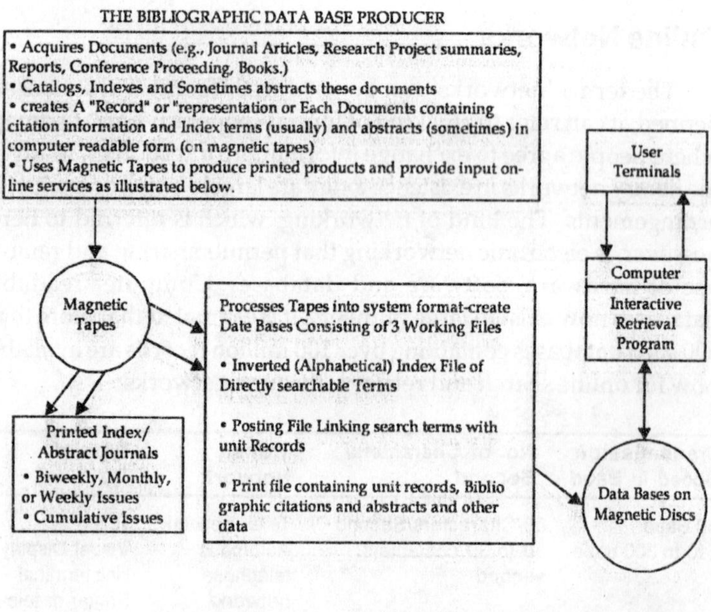

Figure 2.1. Relationship between Data Bases, online Retrieval Services and the Online User

Ten years ago, communication technology for remote use of databases was extremely expensive and not publicly available. Communication networks that now exist include government-sponsored networks (e.g. ESANET of the

European Space Agency) and commercial networks, such as TYMNET, TELENET, TRANSPAC, ITAPAC and so on. In India, Computer Maintenance Corporation Ltd., (CMC) set up INDONET, a data network with mainframe computers installed at New Delhi, Calcutta, Bombay, Pune, Bangalore and Madras and linked to each other through dedicated lines. Databases loaded in any one of the INDONET nodes can be accessed online from remote terminals. CMC is trying to get existing databases from various organizations and make them accessible online through INDONET. They are also setting up an international gateway at Bombay with the cooperation of Videsh Sanchar to enable Indian users to access international databases available from Lockheed/DIALOG, SDC, Orbit, ESANET and so on.

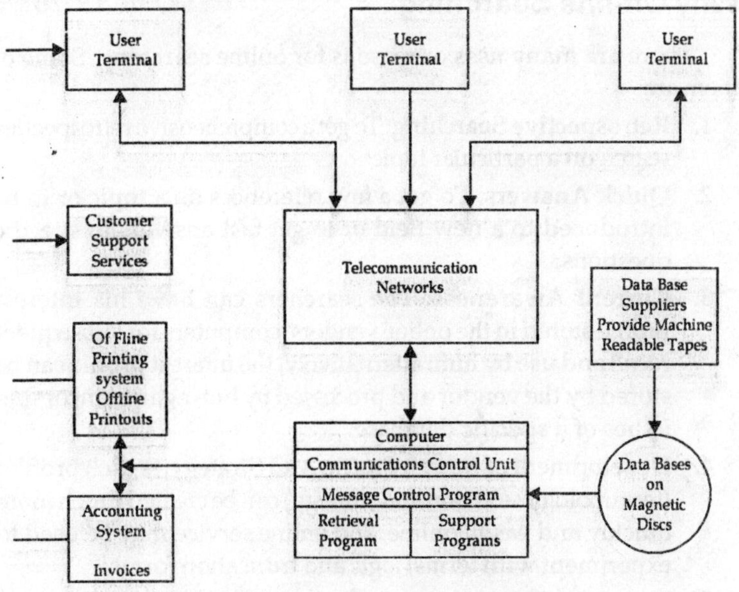

Figure 2.2. Online Retrieval System

When dealing with databases, we must distinguish between the names of communications networks, such as, TYMNET, TELENET etc, and the names of parent organizations that provide database services through these networks, For instance, Lockheed/DIALOG and SDC/Orbit provide online services through TYMNET, Lockheed and SDC obtain various databases from information providers that produce computer accessible informations, such as, the American Chemical Society *(Chemical Abstracts)*, the United Engineering Information Center (COMPENDEX), the American Metals Society (METADEX), the Institution of Electrical Engineers, London, (INSPEC) and so on, and make these databases searchable from their computers and with their own software through the communication networks like TYMNET, TELENET and so on. Figure 1 shows the relationship between databases, online services and the online user and Figure 2.2 illustrates an online retrieval system.

Why On-line Searching

There are many uses or reasons for online searching. Some of them are:

1. **Retrospective Searching:** To get a comprehensive retrospective search on a particular topic;
2. **Quick Answers:** To get a few references on a topic or to be introduced to a new field or to get fast answers to specific questions;
3. **Current Awareness:** The searchers can have his interest profile stored in the online vendors' computers for subsequent recall and use by him; alternatively, the interest profile can be stored by the vendor and processed by him against incoming issues of a specific database;
4. **Development of Search Profile And Strategy:** Search profiles (terminology selection and strategy) can be created much more quickly and easily online; and online service may be used to experiment with terms, logic and truncation forms;
5. **Training:** Online search facilitates the training of personnel in search techniques;
6. **Bibliometric Studies:** Online searching can be used to conduct various types of bibliometric studies of the databases, journal coverage of specific journals etc.;
7. **Online And Offline Printing:** Online systems are useful as printing machines-either online or offline. From printed indexes, one has to copy down, often from tiny print, full

author/title/journal/address details of the required items, often with abstracts as well. Online and offline printing takes the drudgery out of compiling search results in a form useful to the customer;

8. **Access to Occasional Interest Files:** Online systems offer access to files that are peripheral and are only needed on rare occasions. Very few information centers can afford to subscribe to every indexing service they might at some point need from the point of view of economics, space and other factors.

Growth in Online Systems

In the relatively short span of their existence, online systems have already had a great impact upon the scientific, academic and business communities and in the way information is accessed and retrieved. Online services have made available, at lower cost, files whose printed equivalents are beyond the budgets of many organizations. Publishers describe the effect as a migration of users from printed products to their online counterpart.

By the end of this decade, it is envisaged that most workplaces of scientists, administrators and decision-makers will be equipped with a computer terminal linked to a network, which will allow the following possibilities:

1. Communication with any other terminal on the network;
2. Access to numerical, statistical and bibliographic databases and databanks, the last containing full texts;
3. Access to major computational capabilities of the network;
4. Personalized mail, with text and graphics;
5. Distance teaching and other educational services;
6. Electronic shopping for goods and services;
7. News reporting and distribution;
8. Teleconferencing.

Indeed, the possibilities are limitless and these will fundamentally change the way people shop, bank, work and communicate since they can do all of these things without leaving their places. They will be able to call upon their video-screens the news on selected topics, airline schedules, sports events, community developments, stock and commodity prices, weather forecast and a host of other continuously updated information.

Online Network in Europe

The European Space Agency (ESA) is an inter-governmental organization with headquarters at Paris, which promotes cooperation among European States in space research and technology. ESA has several cooperative programmes in space-related activities with NASA in USA and the Indian Space Research Organization (ISRO). Following a successful demonstration of online access to the NASA database from California, USA, via satellite during 1969, ESA started a computer-based Space Documentation Service since 1971 starting with the NASA database. Regular online access services were provided to the member-organizations since 1973.

ESA/IRS is the third largest database operator in the world, after Lock-head/DIALOG and SDC/Orbit and it is the largest online network in Europe. It has a large IBM computer at Frascati, near Rome, Italy, with 6 MB main memory and more than 2 trillion bits of disk space. Its computer is accessible through the public data transmission networks in the various member-states at all standard transmission speeds i.e., 50, 300, 1200 and 2400 bauds, and through telex, videotex terminals, word processors and microcomputers. ESA/IRS has more than 70 databases and databanks include aerospace, agriculture, biotechnology, chemistry, computers, electronics engineering, mechanical engineering, energy, environment, management, mathematics and several other fields including trade and commerce. ESA/IRS has also started to offer access via its computer to other services, for example, to EURONET/DIANE and FINSBURY in UK. It has also extended its services to Rabat in Morocco and Beijing in China by setting up access terminals in these countries.

In the Early Stage

During November 1976, INSDOC had arranged a demonstration of online access to the ESA/IRS databases from terminals installed at Bombay. This project was supported by NISSAT. Following this successful demonstration, INSDOC had submitted a proposal to the Government of India for setting up ESA/IRS terminals in India.

However, due to various factors, this proposal did not materialize at that time.

During 1979-80, an experimental project was undertaken by the Information Center for Aeronautics in NAL, Bangalore, to conduct information searches from the ESA databases on an offline basis. This project was supported by NISSAT with a financial grant of Rs. 75,000 and by ISRO, which is the counterpart agency of ESA in India. Under this project, 51 search queries received from 12 organizations in Bangalore and outside were sent to the ISRO Liaison Officer in Paris for conducting the searches on the ESA terminals and sending the search results to NAL by airmail. An analysis of the feed back received from the users in respect of 28 queries had shown that 61 percent of the references contained in the print outs were found to be relevant.

Online Demonstrations in Bangalore and New Delhi

At the request of NAL, sent through ISRO, ESA had again arranged two demonstrations of online access to its databases from terminals located at Asoka Hotel, New Delhi, and at NAL, Bangalore, from 28th February to 4th March 1981 and from 9th - 11th March 1981 respectively. These demonstrations were similar to the first demonstrations arranged by INSDOC during 1976 and were supported by NISSAT with a grant of Rs.60,000. The demonstration had attracted a large number of scientists, engineers and others and confirmed the technical feasibility of accessing the ESA databases from India through a dedicated telecommuni-cation line provided by the Department of Telecommunica-tions and the Videsh Sanchar of the Government of India.

Implementing the Project

It took nearly three years for NAL to implement the project on the basis of the recommendations of the Expert Committee. During this period, financial support from CSIR, Defense Research and Development Organization (DRDO), Bharat Electronics Ltd., Bangalore, the Aeronautical Development Agency, Bangalore, and the Hindustan Machine Tools Ltd., Bangalore was obtained. Assistance from UNESCO to the extent of $35,000 was also secured to cover the foreign exchange cost of the project. Finally, sanction of the Department of Telecommunications was also obtained for allocating a leased data channel to link the terminals at NAL to the ESA Computer Centre at Frascati via national and international telecommunication network. On 5th June, 1985, ISRO had sent an official request to ESA to set up the facility at NAL. The cost for operating the online facility for one year was estimated to be as under:

Recurring Costs

Data channel Bangalore-Bombay	Rs. 3,50,000 p.a.
Satellite channel Indian portion	Rs. 12,00,000 p.a.
Satellite channel Italian portion	Rs. 12,00,000 p.a.
	Rs. 27,50,000 p.a.

Capital Costs

Cost of equipment (supported by UNESCO)	Rs. 3,00,000
installation, training, maintenance, etc	Rs. 1,50,000
	Rs. 4,50,000
Total costs	**Rs. 32,00,000**

Installation

The facility was installed and commissioned by ESA on 27th June, 1986. The terminal equipment installed at NAL consists of the following:

IBM PC/XT Microcomputer	- 2 Nos.
EMI/NOKIA Modern (2400 bps)	- 2 Nos.
300 lpm printer	- 1 Nos.
180 cps DOT Matrix Printer	- 1 Nos.
X-25 Multipad interface (to operate upto 8 Terminals online simultaneously)	- 1 No.

All these equipments were supplied by UNSECO to NAL.

A schematic diagram showing the telecommunication link connecting the terminals to the ESA Computer is shown in the following figure.

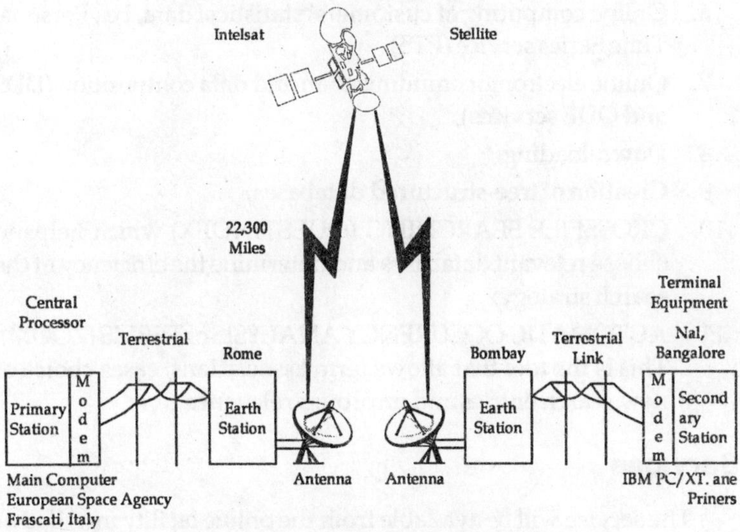

Figure 2.3. Telecommunication Link

Retrieval Software

The software developed by ESA/IRS for online access and retrieval from their databases is known as ESA/QUEST which has a wide range of functions as under:

1. Loading and maintenance of large data files among which CHEMABS and PASCAL, containing 6.5 and 5 million records respectively;
2. Supporting a variety of retrieval languages;
   - ESA/QUEST command language
   - Common Command Language (CCL) both unable on all ESA/IRS databases
   - STAIRS, especially applied in the AGRIS and INIS files
3. Support and control of remote printing stations in various European countries, supplying end users with printed references overnight;
4. Customer accounting;
5. Online current awareness and document ordering facilities (PRIMORDIAL);

6. Online computing of customers' statistical data, i.e., Personal Time Series service (PTS);
7. Online electronic communication and data composition (DDS and ODE services);
8. Down-loading;
9. Creation of tree-structured databases;
10. CROSSFILE SEARCHING (QUESTINDEX) which helps to choose relevant databases and determine the efficiency of the search strategy;
11. AUTOMATIC OCCURENCY ANALYSIS of TERMS (ZOOM). This is the tool that allows term associations, eases choice of new search entries and improves relevance.

Services

The service will be available from the online facility installed at NAL are current awareness services, online ordering of original documents (i.e., we can order xerox reprints of articles from British Library, Boston Spa, online), down-loading, online entry and editing of documents, electronic mail, creation of databases locally and library automation, creation of private files in ESA main computer. The facility is available for use from 9.00 A.M. to 5.00 P.M. on Monday or Friday. Extension of the use of the facility upto 10.00 P.M. is possible.

All Government of India organizations and other organizations supported by Government funds are eligible to use the facility for bonafide research and study only. No commercial use of the facility is permissible. The 'connect-time' costs for accessing the databases will be about Rs.700 per query including online printing upto 50 bibliographic citations. Users can send in details of their search queries by one or more of the following means:

1. By Telex	0845-279 NAL IN
2. By Telephone	574262
3. By Telegram	NAEROLAB, Bangalore
4. By Post	Head, Information Center for Aeronautics National Aeronautical Laboratory P.B. No. 1779 Bangalore–560017, India

Alphabetical List of Files Available on ESA-IRS

Name	No.of File	Main Subject Area	Time Span
ABI/INFORM	30	Management	1971
ABI/SOFT	89	Business Softwares	1983
ACOMPLINE	35	Urban Matters	1973
AEROSPACE DAILY	72	Daily aerospace news	1983
AFEE	73	Aquatic sciences	1970
AGE	70	Geotechnical engineering	1970
AGRIS	29	Agriculture	1975
ALUMINIUM	9	Aluminium	1968
AMPEREDOC	81	Electricity	1983
Time SpanAQUALINE	25	Aquatic environment	1974
BIIPAM	71	Metallurgy	1970
BIOSIS	7	Biology	1973
BRIX	77	Building research	1950
CAB	16	Agriculture	1973
CETIM	54	Engineering	1975
CHEMABS	2	Chemistry	1967
CHEMABS TRAINING	38	Subset of CHEMABS	
CHEMICAL ENGG.	85	Chemical engineering	1970
CIS-DOC	40	Occupational health & safety	1973
COMPENDEX	4	Engineering	1969
CONFER, PAPERS INDEX	36	Conference proceedings	1973
COSMIC	69	Softwares	Current
CURRENT BIOTECH	95	Biotechnology	1983
DATALINE	21	Company profiles	last 5 yrs.
DATASOLVE	104	Political & financial news	last3-5yrs
DELFT HYDRO	91	Hydrology	1977
EDF-DOC	27	Electricity-Energy	1972
EDIN	26	INIS Training Subset	
EI MEETINGS	51	Engineering proceedings	1982
ELECTRONIC MAGAZINE	94	Information sciences	1984
EMIS	105	Materials for electronics	current
ENEL	60	Italian Electricity Board	1980

(Contd.)

Name	No.of File	Main Subject Area	Time Span
ENERGYLINE	19	Energy	1971
ENERGYNET	50	Energy: US key institutions and personnel	1983
ENVIROLINE	11	Environment	1971
EUDISED	24	Educational research projects	1975
FLUIDEX	48	Fluid engineering	1973
FSTA	20	Food sciences	1969
HSELINE	47	Health and safety	1977
IBSEDEX	88	Building research	1979
INIS	28	Nuclear sciences	1975
INSPEC	8	Physics-informatics	1971
INSPEC LIBRARY	31	Information sciences	1971
INSPEC TRAINING	39	Subset of INSPEC	only 1977
IRRD	43	Road research	1972
ISMEC	10	Mechanical engineering	1973
LABORDOC	53	Labour-related aspects	1965
LAB. HAZARDS BULL	90	Chemical hazards	1981
LABOUR INFO.	87	Labour	1974
LEDA	13	Catalogue of remote sensing Images	1975
MASS SPECTR. BULL.	86	Mass spectrometry	1966
MATHSCI	80	Mathematics	1973
MERLIN-TECH	65	Electrical & electronic engineering	1973
METADEX	3	Metallurgy	1969
MOLARS	82	Meterology	1971
NASA	1	Aerospace (access restricted of ESA member states)	1962
NEWSLINE (see also textline)	21	Daily Company news	last 5days
NTIS	6	U.S. government reports	1962
OCEANIC	17	Oceanography	1964
PACKABS	55	Packaging technology	1981
PASCAL	14	Multidisciplinary	1973
PASCAL TRAINING	37	Subset of PASCAL	1976-78
POLLUTION	18	Pollution	1970

Name	No.of File	Main Subject Area	Time Span
ROBOMATIX	84	Robotics	1983
SATELDATA	12	Satellite equip. parameters	1974
SPACECOMPS	22	Components for spacecraft use	1970
STANDARDS & SPECS.	44	U.S. standards & specifications	1950
TELEGEN	49	Bio-engineering	1976
TEXTLINE (see also Newsline)	21	Daily Company news	1980
TRANSDOC	74	Transportation, economic, Policy	1970
WTI	33	Translation announcements	1978

3

Need of Resource Sharing in Libraries

Introduction

Libraries by the score arc searching for the promised land — better services and more materials for the same dollar through resource sharing. Ideology flows into print by the full page, and supports a basic quest for Melville Dewey's practical efficiencies. The purpose of this commentary is not to doubt the faith, the promises it holds, or the systems it supports, but to examine John Fetter man's economic postulate — that library costs are consuming an increasing portion of higher education's budget — and respond to his analysis of causes.

The objectives and the motivating factors are the users' needs interacting with both the very large quantity of library material our culture is accumulating and producing and also the great expense of much of it. The objectives listed lead to the hypothesis that resource sharing is the lifestyle of the future for libraries.

Assigning the computer a major role in information management, Fetterman contends that "the obstacles to resource sharing are no longer inherent in technology, but in people." The National Academy of Sciences report defines the complexity of the problem:

The primary bar to development of national computer-based library and information systems is no longer basically a technology-feasibility problem. Rather it is the combination of complex institutional and organizational human-related problems and the inadequate economic value system associated with these activities. National leadership 10 solve these problems has not emerged.

The core of Fetter man's assessment of the need to share resources is his analysis of the increasing number of dollars spent by libraries during the 1960's. Citing data from The Digest of Educational Statistics, 1970, Fetterman's concludes that

> *the percentage of [the educational] budget for many line matter is decreasing in relation 10 the larger increase for libraries. Only "student aid" (67%) and "sales and services" [144%] have increased to a greater degree than libraries.*
>
> *...The cost of library materials has risen at a rate of between 12% and 25%. This is obviously a considerably higher rate than the cost of living.*

This statement of costs is reviewed here with specific reference to Pennsylvania's academic libraries. The data presented in the following three tables describe the growth and cost of resources and services in Pennsylvania's academic libraries. The percentage comparisons span a four-year period, from 1967 to 1970, when the Consumer Price Index climbed 16. 3%, the prices of United States hardcover books and periodical subscriptions increased 20.2% and 32.9%, respectively, and the publication rate of United States hardcover books rose 25%. This examination of the data indicates that Fetter man's economic analysis is incomplete.

Relationship between Library and Other Educational Services

The meaningful relationship between library and other educational and general (E&G) expenditures is the comparison of library expenditures to the E&G total, a relationship which Fetterman neglects. Library operating expenditures as a percent of the total educational and general expenditures increased only 0.3% (3. 9% to 4.2%) from 1967 to 1970. This 0.3% increase occurred while the following E&G line items also increased: physical plant maintenance, 2.7%; sponsored activities, 4.5%; other, 7.1%. This 4.2% support falls below the ALA Standards for College Libraries which recommend a minimum support of 5.0% of the E&G expenditures for the academic library.

The last columns of Table 2 extend Fetterman's part-to-part analysis of the E&G expenditures to Pennsylvania's statistics. The current-funds expenditures of Pennsylvania's colleges and universities indicate that the costs of Pennsylvania's academic libraries rose 48% between 1967-1968 and 1970-1971 while the category which includes them, E&G expenditures, increased 35%. Library expenditures are increasing more rapidly than other line items such as instruction (30%), but not as rapidly as plant maintenance (76%) or other (329% and 98%) E&G categories. However, this analysis is incomplete, as it does not view library expenditures as a proportion of the total E&G expenditures. When compared to the total E&G expenditures, the 48% increase amounts to the 0.3% increase previously stated. This 0.3% increase is not substantial enough to motivate resource-sharing activities solely on the basis of rapidly rising costs atypical of other E&G expenditures.

The foregoing analysis is incomplete without our acknowledgment of the following factors affecting library costs: technological innovations, inflation, growth of new institutions such as the community college and external degree programs, changes in users' needs and demands for library services, and the unique product that is library services. The major increase in Pennsylvania's library expenditures is for salaries and wages, and covers a period when some significant improvements were made in professional salaries (although library faculty salary scales generally remain below those of the classroom faculty) and wage increases were required to meet minimum wage standards. Although new technologies promise some reduction in labor costs, a study of library economics conducted by William Baumol concludes:

> *One point emerges with special clarity; The nature of library costs is such that they will continue to rise overall, in spite of improved efficiency and cost-reduction efforts. This unavoidable phenomenon must be kept in mind in all future planning if the social value of the 'product' is to be realized.... Just as one cannot reduce without limit, year after year, the amount of faculty time in the educational process, the reduction of librarian time (the growth of the librarian productivity) is also circumscribed by the nature of the activity.*

William Dix, Princeton's librarian, believes that the library's contribution to the educational process justifies increased expenditures for library purposes.

Table 3.1. Selected Categories of Data on Pennsylvania College and University Libraries, with Percent Changes 1967-68 and 1970-71

Items	1967-1968	1970-71	Percent Changes 1967 to 1971 (4 years)
Number of reporting Libraries	144	143	µ
Collections			
Total holdings	20,510,820	29,630,470	+44%
Number of volumes	16,772,579	20,748,399	+24%
Number of microforms	3,508,029	7,083,687	+102%
Library operating expenditures			
Total (excluding capital)	$29,543,396	$41,398,725	+40%
Salaries and wages	$15,138,873	$22,969,241	+52%
Books & library materials	$11,781,438	$14,227,185	+21%
Binding	$1,068,106	$1,245,082	+17%
Other	$1,554,979	$2,957,217	+90%
Distribution of above expenditure			
Total	100%	100%	capital)
Number of volumes	51.2%	55.5%	+4.3%
Books and library materials	39.9%	34.4%	-5.5%
Binding	3.6%	3.0%	-0.6%
Other	5.3%	7.1%	+1.8%
Library operating expenditures as percent of total institutional expenditures for educational & general purposes	3.9%	4.2%	+0.3%
Students served			
Total students enrolled	349,705	411,618	+18%
Number of holdings per student	58.7	72.0	+23%
Library operating expenditures per stndent	$48.48	$100.57	+19%

Table 3.2. Financial Statistics of Pennsylvania Colleges and Universties Current-Funds Expenditures by Function with Percent Changes 1967-1968 and 1970-1971

Item	1967-1968 Dollars	1967-1968 % of total current funds	1970-1971 Dollars	1970-1971 % of total current funds	Percent change 1967-1968 to 1970-1971 (4 years)
Number reporting	138		160		+16%
Total: current funds expenditure	$889,420,414	—	$1,295,749,619	—	+46%
Educational and General: total	698,482,467	78%	946,239,031	73%	+35%
		% of E & G		% of E & G	
Instructional & Debt. research	291,603,130	41.7%	379,671,844	40.1%	+30%
Extension and Public services	13,882,377	2.0%	11,830,478	1.3%	-15%
Libraries	27,011,530	3.9%	39,912,932	4.2%	+48%
Physical plant maintenance	64,884,453	9.3%	113,952,529	12.0%	+76%
Organized ed. dept. activities	63,303,036	9.1%	20,944,396	2.2%	-67%
Organized research	116,378,631	16.7%	106,520,805	11.3%	-8%
Other sponsored activities	14,265,782	2.0%	61,264,533	6.5%	+329%
Other	107,153,528	15.3%	212,141,514	22.4%	+98%
Student aid grants	50,866,681	6%	74,752,208	6%	+47%
Auxiliary enterprises	121,427,830	14%	151,543,381	11%	+25%
Major service programs	—	—	106,855,999	8%	—
Physical plant assets	18,643,436	2%	32,613,015	2%	+75%

If it were possible to measure the source of each bit of education, it just might turn out that the library, even in its present imperfect state, is responsible for as much as half of the educational product.

Dix proposes that a better balance between the library and teaching departments may increase the library's percentage of the E&G expenditures to 10%.

A problem common to both Baumol's study and Dix's observations is that neither is the result of a cost-benefit analysis. Existing data on library operations inadequately describes costs and activities. Many libraries cannot define efficiencies for their users in terms of collection and distribution systems. Consequently, firm answers to the basic question to be asked of any resource-sharing proposal— Can it save money and improve operating efficiencies without transferring a burden of inconveniences or costs to the user? — are unavailable. Better methods of measuring and evaluating services and their benefits must be derived if libraries are to engage in the most beneficial resource sharing activities.

Both the resources to be shared and the mechanics for sharing them cost money. Libraries' critical support needs should be acknowledged. The availability of library funds from colleges and universities depends not only on the incomes and contributions received by these institutions, but are affected by the competing demands of other college activities. The essential nature of a library's information services in an academic community must be recognized in assigning it a high priority in the budget allocation, process. Funding sources must include federal aid because of libraries' importance for the nation's educational and research activity, and relatively modest need in comparison with other claimants upon government resources. Demonstrating this "essential nature" to academic administrators, governments, and foundations depends on the development and employment of adequate methods of evaluating the effectiveness of library services.

Fetterman directs us to "face the problem"– library costs and publication rates versus self-sufficiency. The answer are complex. There is a wide range of functions, sizes, sources of financing and operational environments for libraries and their interfacing information production and demand activities. The National Academy of Sciences Report acknowledges:

Table 3.3. Price Indexes and Book Production

	1967	1970	1971
Consumer price index			
All items	100.0	116.3	121.3
Library materials index			
U.S. hardcover books	100.0	120.2	134.6
Average price	$8.77	$11.66	$11.6
U.S. periodicals	100.0	132.9	151.0
Average price	$8.77	$11.66	$13.25
U.S. book title output			
Output Index	100.0	125.0	131.0
Number	28,762	36,071	37,692

Acceptable costs in one situation are not tolerable in another. Nor does the appropriate operating mode for a small library provide the same unit cost and functional performance as for a huge library. Similarly, the method appropriate for serving a graduate student doing original research is not necessarily the same as quick-response support for a business executive. Or the instructional support needed for an undergraduate.

The demands of the curriculum for on-campus resources challenge the theory of, resource sharing in the academic arena. A college curriculum is the domain of the faculty and their disciplines, and the faculty expect the library to provide the supporting books and journals on its shelves. Fetter-man touches the problem briefly when he states, "Thousands of dollars are being myopically committed because College A, located very close to College B, does not know that the one is developing a curriculum in the same expensive support area as the other," The catch hero is to define, then to control "unnecessary duplication" in curricular offerings - a problem of considerable complexity, and one beyond the reach of the libraries. Enlisting the support of the academic community requires administrative leadership as well as some proof of resource sharing's benefits.

Union catalogs, union lists, and delivery systems are operating successfully in various parts of the state, acquisitions agreements are beginning to emerge in some cooperative units, and CRT terminals to the Ohio College Library Center system are in use in a number of Pittsburgh and Philadelphia area libraries (although current costs of the OCLC system restrict its affordability). The problems faced by Pennsylvania's libraries are common to all libraries searching for the means to meet the information requirements of today's society. To practice the ideology of resource sharing, librarians must discover how to achieve reasonable standards, remain fiscally solvent, avoid unnecessary redundancy, maintain intellectual and other kinds of freedoms, provide for utility and convenience to the user, for rational diversity, for flexibility, for sound design - and at the same time avoid the creation of a monster.

4

Methods and Techniques of Library Resource Sharing

Overview

Resource sharing has been analyzed from four-library operations acquisitions, cataloging and processing, storage libraries, and the delivery of services. At the end of each section below a sequence of goals is stated. If these goals are taken separately they may be part of a cooperative resource-sharing consortium; however, if these goals, as well as possible additional ones not mentioned, are developed concurrently a centralized resource-sharing consortium could result. These goals are:

1. Statement of the mission and objectives of the consortium
2. A common materials selection program
3. A specific statement of the optimum consortium collection
4. A union catalog of all materials
5. A union desiderata list
6. A common request and order form for all libraries in the system
7. A central order office
8. A union on-order/in-process file
9. A consortium approval plan

10. Cooperative circulation of want lists of out-of-print material
11. Cooperative ordering of photographic or microform copies of material
12. A consortium exchange program
13. Use of the ISBD for all consortium cataloging
14. Consortium participation in or development of a MARC-based centralized cataloging center (which could be a part of item 20)
15. A centralized original cataloging unit (which could be a part of item 20)
16. Use of LC subject headings by all member libraries
17. Consistent use centrally of classification systems – possible use of only LC classification (another part of item 20)
18. A centralized original subject-cataloging unit (including classification and subject headings) (another part of item 20)
19. A union shelf list
20. A centralized processing unit (possibly containing items 7, 14, 15, 1 7 and 18)
21. A consortium storage library
22. A union catalog of the storage library
23. A consortium agreement on the use priorities of stoı ed material
24. A possible consortium exchange agreement for stored material
25. A clearly stated policy on the amount of time to retrieve material from storage
26. A consortium interlibrary loan system
27. A possible consortium SDI system
28. A consortium teletype network
29. A common circulation system
30. A consortium delivery system
31. A common library card (or reciprocal borrowing privileges)

A final and central concern is the difficulty of establishing within each institution, among faculty and students especially, an understanding of the dimensions of the fiscal crisis and the implications of steps to deal with it, both immediately and in the long term. The habits of students and faculty and their expectations for resources and services within their own institutions will have to be modified if constraints on collection growth are to be effectual in some libraries, if access to selected resources is to be extended to individuals from other institutions, and if special aspects of "custom-made" records and services arc going to be sacrificed in favor of mass produced and, hence uniform products.

> *...no library, whether it be one sharply focused on limited institutional needs or one containing wide ranging research collections, is self sufficient. The process of instruction has no distinct boundaries limiting absolutely the resources required, nor does research preclude a need for certain basic and fundamentul materials.*

Introduction

Our purpose here is to examine simply and theoretically the basic library operations: acquisitions, processing, storage, and delivery of services. First, these operations will be examined in regard to their execution within an individual or separate library; second, they will be considered in regard to any differences in their execution that might occur in resource sharing or library cooperation. For our purposes the phrase -"resource sharing" will be treated as a specific euphemism for "library-cooperation. "Within the literature of this subject the words "cooperation," "centralization," "consortium," "network," and "resource sharing" are not consistently or precisely employed. A group of libraries working together in a cooperative manner may be called a consortium, a library network or resource sharing system. We will use these three terms interchangeably. However, a. clear distinction must be drawn between "cooperation" and "centralization, "A cooperative system or network can exist without central headquarters. It may, in fact, be decentralized. A centralized system or network implies the existence of central headquarters. Herman M. Weisman cites the advantages of the two approaches: "Centralization offers the advantages of greater efficiency, economy, and availability of full resources of-the system to many and every component of users. The advantages of decentralization are quicker, direct, and personalized services.

We further propose to demonstrate that the technical processes for resource sharing do exist and have in fact existed for some time. The basic problem is willingness of libraries and their parent institutions to cooperate even if local independence is weakened or lost. Can libraries and their parent institutions continue to be independent and self-sufficient and not rely on other libraries and institutions in the locality or region? Can the spirit of cooperation be coexistent with the stated mission and goals of the parent institution? Must one's own community of users be served first and best? Can libraries and their parent institutions afford the increasing costs of redundancy? What services can libraries afford to make available to non-institutional users? What is the priority or priorities of service among administration, faculty, graduate students, undergraduate students, non-institutional users? These are questions that must be asked, considered, and answered before a successful system of resource sharing can exist.

An all-important. overriding question is just how far are we willing to go to develop a resource-sharing consortium. When the mission and objectives of such a consortium are written and accepted by its members, will these determine if the consortium is to be more important than any single member or will it be equal to a member library or will it be less important than any single member? Further, it must be asked if cooperation can succeed without centralization of some activities. For our purposes here it will be assumed that, at least theoretically, cooperation is one aspect of and may lead to centralization and/or federation — or even incorporation.

> *One of the reasons for reluctant engagement in network development should be concentrated in one or a few institutions While such reasoning is perhaps true with respect to some overall aspects of the network development, it does not apply to the vast amount of procedural aspects that will always remain the prerogative and the responsibility of the individual institution. This largely applies also to the concept of sharing computer programmes, a concept frequently quoted but seldom materialized.*
>
> *The expanding information media, the mounting cost of acquisition of these materials, the magnitude of the acquisition and controlling-effort associated with these materials and the progressively more universal orientation of information service force upon us the concept of network, and we have to be prepared to deal with it and to accept the challenge of closing the information circuit.*

A more concise statement may be the following single sentence from a paper written by Samuel Lazerow, chairman of the National Libraries Task Force on Automation at the Library of Congress, "The excellence of American Libraries over the years has rested in a large measure upon the extent to which cooperative enterprises have been successfully undertaken" One of Kilgour's justifications for the Ohio College Library Center seems to be particularly pertinent to the development of an academic Library consortium in Pennsylvania:

> *Early formulation of the problem that the Ohio College Library center is to solve had occurred in a general way before the Center became a corporate entity. Put succinctly, the problèm to be solved was one of increasing resources to Ohio colleges and universities. From the college administrative point of view, the problem was that of hiring new faculty and enrolling new students in the future. Presidents of Ohio academic institutions were particularly aware that new Ph. D.'s are research-oriented. If these younger men are not offered an opportunity to pursue research programs, they are reluctant to join a faculty. Moreover, changing educational objectives in colleges are requiring that undergraduates have an increasing opportunity to learn how to learn. Such opportunities can best be given to a student by providing him with resources for independent work.*

Library Material

Although libraries handle a wide variety of types of materials of both a print and nonprint nature, this paper will deal specifically with examples of general print material with only occasional examples and uses of various special materials. Specifically monographic material (as librarians often call books) will be used in this paper as examples. A monograph may be defined as a work collection or other writing dealing with a particular subject or subjects. A monograph is usually self contained and not dependent upon other publications. Serial materials will also be considered as a primary type of general library materials, Serials are defined as publications issued in successive installments at regular or irregular intervals and intended to continue indefinately. Periodicals are one common type of serials. A work may be considered to be a periodical if it is not cataloged and classified and if it is simply arranged alphabetically with other periodicals or magazines. Nonperiodical serials are cataloged and classified and shelved with the monographic collection. Pamphlets are a special type of library material which is not cataloged or classified but rather filed alphabetically by subject.

There are many other types of materials which may be called special materials either because of their physical form (nonprint) or because of their special print nature (documents, manuscripts, maps, music, etc.). Nonprint materials include phonograph records, motion picture films, film strips, microforms, pictures, photographs, slides and all forms of machine readable data and records. An administrative decision within each library must be made in regard to cataloging and/or classifying each of these special materials. Very often libraries will catalog special materials but not classify them. As most special materials cannot be physically shelved with the corresponding book materials, a book classification system may not be applied to them. How a library handles these special materials is most important in relation to developing any resource sharing or library Cooperation among a group of libraries. This is a particularly important point as this type of material is very often handled differently by different libraries.

Print materials include rare books, government documents, archival material, manuscripts, globes, maps, atlases, and music. These special materials are often processed in a different fashion from the general print material. The cataloging may be more extensive as in the case of rare books, or less extensive as in the ease of government documents.

Acquisitions

This unit will deal with the selection of materials, acquisition processes such as searching and ordering, and receipt and record keeping. The writer fully realizes that many specific functions will be defined in this section and the following sections and that although many of the readers of the paper are already quite aware of these functions their definitions and distinctions are included to provide the n on library participants at the conference the basic information that they will need in order to contemplate the problems of resource sharing. The writer also fully realizes that this section and the following sections will have to generalize many of the basic library functions and not go into specifics or many specific examples. For the sake of this section acquisitions may be defined as all those processes involved in deciding, ordering, and receiving materials into a library's collection.

Selection (Maintenance and Development)

Selection involves the maintenance and development of the materials selection program, the handling of specific requests for material not in the collection, and the criteria for the decision to acquire such material. In addition the processes of searching the library catalog to determine whether or not the requested material is already in the collection and verification of the existence bibliographically of requested material are processes related to selection,

Materials Selection Program

A materials selection program consists of the following functions and may be considered as an organic substitute for a book selection policy. The first basic function of such a program is an analysis of the community to be served by the library. The mission and objectives of a parent institution must be used to determine the initial limits of the library. The user groups to be serviced by the library must be identified. Further, the priorities of the user groups and services to them must be established.

The influences of the budget, the curriculum, and past practices must be taken into account and the nature of the service to be rendered by the collection must be clearly stated. This would also have a major effect on any library involved in a resource sharing system. Resource sharing immediately expands the potential user group of an individual library and may expand the nature of service to be rendered and certainly priorities for the user groups must be taken into consideration.

At this point we must face the basic question of any possible consortium or resource sharing system or network. Simplistically speaking is the local library with its community of users to be given greater, equal or lesser priority than the total community of users of the consortium? Further, can the missions and objectives of the individual parent institutions be made to articulate with the mission and objectives of the entire consortium? Every effort should be made to allow the statement of mission and objectives of the consortium to be in harmony with the missions and objectives of the individual parent institutions. For example, cooperative use of library resources may be compared with, but hopefully not equalled to, existing cross registration systems of academic institutions. In all events, for a cooperative materials selection program to be considered, the consortium must have a clear statement of its mission and objectives.

The ideal priority may be to have all potential users on an equal basis, but, realistic considerations, including budgetary commitments, may force local priorities to have precedence.

Sarah Katherine Thompson in the preface to the Interlibrary Loan Procedure-Manual discusses possible priorities of interlibrary loan service which may be applicable to an entire consortium operation:

Every library has the right to specify conditions of loan and to decline to lend specific materials. Each lending library has an obligation to establish priorities of user demands upon its collections. In general, these priorities are:

1. **Public library:** (a) its community; (b) other libraries in its system; (c) other libraries in the same state; (d) out of state libraries.
2. **College library:** (a) its faculty, students, research, staff; (b) local community, other libraries in its system; (c) other academic libraries; (d) libraries in general.
3. **University library:** (a) its faculty, students, research, staff; (b) other libraries in its system, academic and research personnel in its area; (c) other academic libraries; (d) other libraries.
4. **Special library:** (a) personnel of its organization; (b) affiliated organizations; (c) other special libraries and university libraries from which it borrows; (d) other libraries.

The next phase of any materials selection program includes the influence of the analysis of the community on the statement of the nature of the services, that is to say, the service policy. This must be considered in relation to the optimum collection of materials. This ideal collection of materials should be specified. First, subject areas of the collection must be indicated. The type of material in each area should be determined; the quality and quantity of material in each subject area should be given careful consideration. Second, the priorities of the service policy and the environmental characteristics must be used as collection building criteria. Third, any special collections should be designated and justified in a resource sharing system. For instance, if one library assumes the responsibility for building a particular subject area not only for its own users but for the entire system, this must be taken into account. The fourth significant point in a material selection program is the analysis of the existing collections in relation to the optimum or desired collection and the collection specifications. This analysis will determine the current selection needs. It must be remembered that such a materials selection program is a continuous one, recognizing and adapting to any changes in the priorities of the library or the parent institution or the resource sharing consortium.

The optimum collection of materials for a consortium should be specified. At least the existing areas of specialization must be indicated. Just as with the individual library, the subject areas should be indicated first.

If this activity is selected by a consortium, the decision to be made is "What areas should each college or university specialize in?" One difficulty that arises is that this decision, involves the faculty and presidents of the institutions, and affects - and is affected by - the curriculum of the institutions, An academic library cannot extensively delimit its collection, unless the college or university delimits its teaching program. A professor of African history and literature may be displeased to learn that the library will not collect beyond the minimal level in this subject area; however, his displeasure may be alleviated if he knows that another consortium member has been able to develop a comprehensive collection in African history and literature, to which he has not only bibliographical access as the result of consortium exchange of bibliographies, but also physical access, in that a truck delivery system will bring him the book he requests within 24 hours.

A library certainly need not buy the most specialized research materials if its clientele has ready access to them at another library in the locality; every library should, where possible, seek cooperative agreements of this kind which will increase its purchasing power, reduce the competition for scarce material, and further scholarship. Second, no library should expect another to bear the burden of its needs except for the rare, the unusual, and the relatively little used. A few university libraries, on both sides of the Atlantic, readily admit that they do not have, on the average, 40-80 percent of the titles required for a dissertation. The justification for these universities offering work for the doctor's degree seems dubious. And third, the extent to which a library can afford not to acquire specialized research materials in fields of concern to its scholars, varies indirectly as the distance to a library which has those materials. No reasonable man will object to having to spend two hours in travel, or waiting a day or two (Princeton to Philadelphia or New York, Mainz to Frankfurt, Ann Arbor to Detroit, Stanford to Berkeley, Bonn to Cologne) once or twice a year. He will object mightily if he is asked to do so once or twice a week, and rightly so. And the greater and oftener his expenditure of time or the delay, the greater his objection.

The existing materials selection policies of the individual libraries should be collected and carefully analyzed and coordinated if possible. Further, the existing collections must be evaluated in relation to the proposed optimum consortium collection as well as the previously determined collection specifications. In order to do this evaluation most effectively the consortium may need to generate a union catalog of all the member libraries in the consortium. Further, the results of this evaluation and analysis should generate a union list of desired materials. As the suggestion for a union catalog will recur in each of the following sections, it is appropriate to discuss the meaning and potentials of a union catalog for a consortium.

A Union Catalog. Silvere Willemin defines a union catalog in his Technique of Union Catalogues: A Practical Guide: "A union catalogue is an inventory common to several libraries and containing all or some of their publications listed in one or more orders of arrangement". He further cites the following bibliographical functions for a union catalog.

Types of Union Catalogue

The main function of the union catalogue is unquestionably to locate publications in order to facilitate access to books. It is a tool for the rationalization of interlibrary loans.

The second function derives from the foregoing and is to transform the union catalogue into the nucleus of a bibliographical research center by reason of the identification work required for the sound operation of both inter-library and international loans.

Thirdly, the bibliographical center which is essential to the sound operation of the union catalogue tends ultimately to become also a bibliographical information service carrying out a variety of tasks.

Ruth Patrick in her Guidelines for Library Cooperation discerns five different types of union catalogs and lists: (1) complete union catalogs; (2) selective union catalogs and lists; (3) exchange of acquisition lists, catalog cards, or bibliographies; (4) lists of collection resources of the member libraries; (5) union list of serials A complete union catalog would contain all the monographic holdings of the member libraries. Patrick points out:

> *To produce a union catalog of the retrospective holdings of several large libraries would be an expensive undertaking. The advisable strategy on this activity seems to be to wait until the Library of Congress or the larger academic libraries have converted their retrospective holdings into machine-readable form, and to use their records instead of keyboarding the same bibliographic data in each individual library,*

Selective union catalogs and lists may be limited to special subject areas or collections of importance or may be limited to current material that has been processed centrally for the consortium. The possible exchanges of acquisition lists, catalog cards and bibliographies represent another form of a selective union catalog or list. The benefits and the cost of maintenance or exchanging the acquisition lists and catalog cards are open to serious question. The exchange of microfilm copies of individual library catalogs could be far more valuable. The exchange of locally produced bibliographies can have more potential merit. Patrick states:

> *Members of several consortia reported they felt it was useful to exchange bibliographies compiled by member libraries. A bibliography on a topic of current interest, such as ecology, may be of use to librarians as a selection tool, as well as to users seeking material on the topic. But in order to be of assistance to the users, bibliographic access would ideally have to be accompanied by physical access to the materials, such as could be made available through reciprocal borrowing previleges or expanded interlibrary loan.*

Lists of collection resources of the member libraries may be seen as another mechanism related to union catalogs and lists. Patrick defines this:

> *As a partial substitute for a complete union catalog or list. One benefit of this activity is that it can facilitate inter-library loans: Instead of indicating a specific book that a library owns, it indicates the subject areas in which the libraries are strong. For example, if a library has a strong collection on the subject of education, other members will know, if they receive an interlibrary loan request for a book in this subject area, that there is a good chance of locating it at this particular library.*

Another value of this activity is that a list of this kind does not take as long to produce as a union catalog, and this is a comparatively quick way of learning what is in the collections of the consortium libraries. Librarians reported that they learn of collection strengths in other member libraries of which they had been unaware previously. In one consortium that consisted of small college libraries only, librarians reported that they now consulted each other for inter-library loan requests, whereas before they had always consulted larger library on the assumption that the small libraries would not have the requested book. Although consortium activities have not made these libraries entirely self-sufficient, their interaction with consortium members has, to a certain degree, lessened their dependency on larger libraries.

A fifth type of union catalog is the union list of serials. This is one of the most common developments for a resource sharing system. Patrick discusses this in the following:

> *The union list of serials can consist of serials or periodicals of all subject fields, or it can be limited to special subjects or to newspapers. It can be used for interlibrary loan by providing users with information about the resources of the consortium libraries. It can also guide librarians to plan more complete coverage of serials and to help avoid unnecessary acquisition of low-use items already by consortium members.*

Large libraries sometimes complain about smaller libraries overusing their resources. One explanation may be that it is mainly the large libraries that are listed in the national union lists. Once smaller libraries have union lists of their own resources, they can be less of a burden on the large libraries. Librarians of several smaller libraries in our sample stated that once they learned of the library holdings of other consortia members of about the same size, they consulted them more often than before the union list had been compiled.

The major union catalogs in the United States include the "following in approximate order of size holdings: the National Union Catalog at the Library of Congress; the Bibliographical Center for Research, Rocky Mountain Region, Inc. at Denver; The Pacific Northwest Bibliographic Center at the University of Washington; the Union Library Catalogue of Pennsylvania in Philadelphia; the Cleveland Regional Union Catalog in the Case Western Reserve University; the Union Catalog of the State Library of Ohio in Columbus;

the Nebraska Union Catalog in Lincoln; the Union Catalog at the California State Library in Sacramento; the Union Catalog of the Atlanta-Athens area in Atlanta; the North Carolina Intel-library Center at the University of North Carolina; the Vermont Free Public Library Service at Montpelier; the Union List of New Hampshire Libraries in Concord; and the Union Catalogue of Books in Nashville Libraries. Obviously in Pennsylvania any consortium proposal must carefully consider the potentials of the Union Library Catalogue of Pennsylvania.

Demand for Material

Normally, individual materials to lie selected result from a request for such material. Such a request for an individual monograph or serial may be made by a faculty member, a student, a librarian, or other user of a library. Basic bibliographic information concerning the requested material should be received at this time; such information normally includes the title of the material, the author if one exists, the publisher, the place of publication, the date of publication, and the sources of the material; that is to say how the requester came upon this particular item. Libraries forming a resource sharing system would also need to determine whether or not requests could be accepted from other member libraries and from other users from other member libraries. This, of course, can lead to the use of a common request form for all libraries in the system. A common request form is simply one example of the many forms of standardization which may be necessary for a consortium to operate effectively. The standardization of cataloging will be discussed in the next main section. The following quotation from Leonard,. Maier, and Dougherty is generally applicable to any form of centralization within a consortium.

Standardization of many of the participants' processing routine is a significant element in the design and successful implementation of centralized book processing. Exception procedures resulting from lists of local modifications may well render a center ineffective and uneconomical. Establishment of a set of well defined, workable specifications is the only realistic approach to the organization and operation of a processing center.

The next step in the process is a selection decision. The library must decide if the requested material should fit into the collection according to the material selection program and if the library can presently afford to purchase the material, If the library wishes to purchase the material but cannot at that time, the request may be filed for later consideration. If the library can afford the material and wishes to purchase it, the next step is searching. In a resource sharing system, libraries may wish to consider whether or not other member libraries have the material available rather than purchasing it themselves.

Searching is, simply, checking to see if the library already has a copy of the requested book in its collection or if a copy of the requested book is already on order from a publisher or dealer. Further, the library may wish in a resource sharing system to determine if other member libraries have acquired or are buying the requested material. Again we may see the potential use of a union catalog for the consortium. If a copy of a requested title is already held by a member library, the immediate request may be fulfilled more quickly than by ordering and processing a copy for the individual library. This will also allow the requesting library to examine and evaluate the further potential uses of requested material by examining the copy in hand.

Verification

Verification is the next step in the process. Verification means checking in some standard bibliographic source to see if the book or other requested material really exists and if the information about the material is correct. Is the author's name in correct form? Is the title correct? Who is the publisher? When was the book published? How much does the book cost? If there are any changes in the information about the book in this step the request must be searched again. Again a union catalog would be helpful in the verification process.

Acquisitions Processing

Acquisitions processing involves an analysis of the type of material to be ordered or otherwise acquired. Material may be "in-print" or "out-of-print" or may be available by exchange agreement or may be given to the library' as a gift. If material is currently available from a publisher it is called "in-print" material. Such material may be ordered in the following fashion.

Ordering

Each copy of a piece of material may be ordered separately. This is often called "title-by-title" ordering. The individual titles may be ordered direct from the individual publisher or other direct sources. In order to avoid separate billing libraries may place a group or batch of orders through a dealer or jobber who buys in bulk from many publishers. Such jobbers may be national, regional, or local. There are in most cases two types of local jobbers, commercial and institutional. Many academic libraries order some or all of their material through the local campus book store in a potential resource sharing system libraries could go into bulk or batch ordering by mutual agreement as such ordering might reduce the cost of material.

A centralized order office for the consortium would facilitate this step. This could also lead to a centralized order record file. The other uses of such a file may be seen in the following discussions.

Even if a centralized order office is not initially established, consortium members can develop a system of prepurchase checking. Patrick discusses some possibilities in this.

Materials may be ordered automatically if some form of standing order is used. The most common form of standing order is subscription to serial publications. Once such an order has been placed the order continues until it is cancelled. Such orders may be placed either with publishers directly or through serials jobbers. Further blanket order plans may be placed with some publishers for all of their publications or for all of their publications in a specific series. A blanket order plan provides an approach to monographic acquisitions that is similar to serial subscriptions. A third type of standing order plan is the approval plan. In an approval plan the profile of an individual library is analyzed and material within that profile is automatically sent to the library "on approval." As most approval plans require that libraries pay return costs, libraries try to select carefully their designated profile with the operator of an approval plan. The profile must carefully consider the collections specifications of the individual library. As a result there could be serious difficulties to be considered in applying a resource sharing concept directly to approval plans. Approval plans are available from publishers, jobbers, and dealers. There are approval plans for special subject areas as well as specific foreign material.

It is, of course possible to have an approval plan profile developed for the entire consortium. Such a plan would naturally evolve from the previously mentioned material selection program for the consortium. There could be central or regional locations for the display of approval material for all members of the consortium. Further, both the individual libraries and the consortium could possibly maintain separate approval plan systems for carefully specified areas and/or categories of material.

When material is no longer currently available from a publisher, it is called "out-of-print." Such material may be acquired in the following ways: The most common sources for "out-of-print" material are dealers in used or rare books. Although libraries in a resource sharing system may be in competition for the same material, there could be cooperative circulation of want lists to selected dealers as well as cooperative advertising in journals dealing with book collecting. A second possible approach to this type of material is having a photographic copy made. Often such a copy is done on microfilm or some other microform. There could, of course, be cost savings in this approach by the production of multiple copies for a resource sharing network. In addition, if a book is in great demand it may be reprint by a publisher specializing in limited reprint editions. Often such an edition is far more expensive than the original edition or the microform edition. Finally, some libraries have acquired many "out-of-print" and desired titles by purchasing an entire collection either from a dealer or collector. Such purchases usually cover a specific subject and may cause duplication with the current collection.

Interchange of Documents

Material may be acquired by trading or exchanging other material with another institution or by receiving gifts. If an institution produces locally a scholarly serial or series, such may be exchanged with other institutions. In addition, many libraries offer unwanted duplicates for exchange. This may be done by circulating lists of titles available for exchange or by maintaining duplicate shelves. Such an approach means that one library may choose the unwanted duplicates of another library. This would be a particularly appropriate relationship, for a group of libraries in a resource sharing system. Such relations cause exchange agreements to be developed.

Exchange agreements may be established on an item by item exchange, i.e., a one for one approach, or on a priced exchange in which service charges for exchange privileges are developed. A third type of agreement is an open exchange, i.e., one copy of everything published is exchanged Gifts provide another method of acquiring material in a library. Some libraries may be the official depository library for a governmental or professional type of material. This is often true of government documents collections. Gifts may be solicited from local groups and local individuals. If a local individual has an extensive private collection, he may give it to a local library after he no longer needs or uses it. Local authors may be encouraged to deposit their manuscripts. Further, many libraries annually receive unsolicited gifts of varying value.

Centrally, a consortium could maintain exchange programs both with the individual member libraries and with other libraries. In possible conjunction with a central storage library for the consortium, there could be a common housing for unwanted duplicates and other material from member libraries. The consortium could then operate in a fashion similar to the United States Book Exchange.

Quite possibly the consortium book exchange could develop programs the United States Book Exchange program as well as the existing exchange of duplicates programs of major American libraries, especially the program at the Library of Congress.

Receipt and Records

The necessary acquisitions records and their maintenance in relation to the receipt of material complete the acquisitions process of a library. The records developed for "in-print" material must be related to and generated from the approach used to order the material. If a "title by title" approach is employed, the individual record may consist of an individual order letter, an individual order form, a multiple copy order form or even an automated order record. At all events these records must have different arrangements, For searching purposes order records must be arranged by author or title of the material already ordered. For claiming purposes some sort of publisher or source approach is necessary. Further, for invoicing purposes an arrangement by order number is useful. For this reason many libraries use multiple copy order forms. In addition, catalog card information may be ordered at the same time that the individual material is ordered. Cards may be ordered from the Library of Congress or from a regional system. This may change to some extent as publishers include more "Cataloging-in-Publication" information on the verso of the title page. Finally, such a system requires that the records are cleared upon the receipt of both the material and any catalog card information. Outstanding orders must be discerned and material claimed or the order cancelled. There may be possibilities for the use of union order files for a centralized system. Records for standing order material are simpler to maintain once a standing order has been placed. In this case the major problem is the receipt of the ordered material. Items must be checked in when they arrive. Approval plan and blanket order plan material requires rejecting and returning some titles. Cataloging information such as catalog cards must be ordered for all monographic material acquired by standing order plans. Outstanding orders, i.e., material not acquired, must be claimed. Records for exchange material and gifts often cause these two types of material to be more costly than it might seem. Records of the individual exchange agreement must be maintained and used. The conditions of the individual agreements must be fulfilled and the agreed-upon material received. Records must be kept in regard to what was sent and received whether a priced, piece for piece, or open exchange is in effect. Outstanding exchange material must be claimed. Gift and exchange agreements must continue to be negotiated or renegotiated. Gift material must be acknowledged. Unsolicited gifts may need to be rejected, exchanged or sold.

Summary

In summary it may be said that the acquisitions processes arc basically the same for libraries whether they are buying solely for themselves or whether they are in a resource sharing arrangement. There arc, however, some basic activities of a resource sharing consortium that must be implemented if the cooperative procedures are to be productive: first, the services to be rendered by the collections to other member libraries must be clearly defined. This would usually involve budgetary commitments. Second, the cooperating irstutitions would have to establish a basic materials budget however high or low as a minimum on which the consortium could count in order to assure that an adequate body of materials would be maintained and augmented regularly be each of the member libraries. Further budgetary commitments would need to be made on materials which might be bought primarily for the use of the member libraries and not the local library. Third, for resource sharing and acquisitions to be completely productive, a form of clearinghouse would be needed. Union catalogs and union lists would provide a record of the holdings of the member libraries; it may also be necessary for some form of on-order/in-process file to be held in a union fashion so that member libraries would know if someone else already had ordered a book. Obviously, in a resource sharing system so far as acquisitions go individual steps could be taken before centralized acquisitions went into effect.

In conclusion, a centralized acquisitions program should include the following if a resource sharing consortium is to be most effective:

1. Statement of the mission and objectives of the consortium
2. *A* common materials selection program
3. A specific statement of the optimum consortium collection
4. A union catalog of all materials including a union list of serials
5. A union desiderata list
6. A common request and order form for all libraries in the system
7. A central order office
8. A union or central on-order/in-process file
9. A consortium approval plan
10. Cooperative circulation of want lists of out-of-print material.

Cataloging and Processing

This unit will include descriptive cataloging, subject cataloging and preparation of material for the shelves. Just as we have seen in the previous section, these processes are basically the same whether one is dealing with a single library or a consortium. In the following discussion, however, it may be observed that certain local autonomies may have to be sacrificed if a consortium wishes to develop cooperation or centralized cataloging and processing. In this section just as in the preceeding section on acquisitions the writer fully realizes that many specific functions will be defined that readers of this paper are already quite aware of; however, these definitions are included to provide the non-library participants with basic library information.

Descriptive Cataloging

Descriptive cataloging consists of generating the necessary descriptive information about the material for the library's catalog. Such information includes the established form of the author's name, the title of the material, any necessary edition statement, the place, publisher and date of publication. This information may already exist on a printed catalog card, or as Cataloging-in-Publication information on the verso of the title page of the material, or may have to be originally generated by the cataloger.

Bibliographic Description

Any bibliographic description will contain certain common elements such as the author and the title of the being described. Bibliographic descriptions or citations may be found in bibliographies, footnotes, indexes, publishers' catalogs, and on library catalog cards. In order to prepare the necessary descriptive information for catalog cards it is necessary to identify and describe certain prescribed parts of books and other material. The basic elements of a bibliographic description of a book, i.e., a monograph, are the title, the edition, the place of publication, the publisher, the date of publication and/or the copyright date, the number of pages of the book, the type of illustrations, the height of the book, any necessary notes, and all possible entries in the catalog including the author, the editor, any joint authors, and any other desired access or index points in the catalog.

By specifying the elements which should comprise a bibliographical description and by prescribing the order in which they should be presented and the punctuation by which they should be demarcated, it aims at three objectives; to make records from different sources interchangeable; to facilitate their interpretation across language barriers; and to facilitate the conversion of such records to machine-readable form.

Library of Congress Cataloging

All the information necessary for a bibliographic description may have already been developed for the cataloger by the Library of Congress or some other bibliographic agency. The cataloger should check to discern if there is Library of Congress cataloging information available for the book being cataloged. This information may exist on Library of Congress printed cards, proof sheets, MARC tapes, or as CIP information on the back of the title page, or as an entry in the Library of Congress[1] printed National Union Catalog.

Many libraries order Library of Congress catalog cards at the same time they order a book. The cataloger must check to see if Library of Congress cards have been ordered and if these printed cards have already arrived. If the cards have been ordered but have not yet arrived the cataloger must decide if temporary cataloging should be done. In some cases libraries simply allow the book to wait for its printed LC cards. After the cards arrive they should be compared with the book to make sure they match the book m all the bibliographic characteristics.

The bibliographic information may be available on MARC tapes, i.e., Machine Readable Cataloging records on magnetic tapes; not all cataloging records at the Library of Congress are presently available on MARC tapes, but all current English language monographs are. In 1973, French language entries have been added to MARC records. Libraries may purchase or subscribe to the tapes or may participate in regional or commercial processing centers which have MARC tapes available. This is one of the most natural areas in cataloging for resource sharing. Henriette Avram, the principal developer of MARC, describes this computer-based system:

The MARC Distribution Service grew out of a pilot project to test the feasibility of centrally producing and distributing machine-readable catalog records, The First Conference on Machine-Readable Catalog Copy in 1964, attended by representatives of the Library of Congress, universities, research agencies, government agencies, and private industry. Consensus was that early availability of machine-readable catalog copy as a by-product of LC's cataloging operations would be desirable. Since the record, would be used for a variety of purposes in many libraries, agreement on data elements to be encoded was desirable, and the design of the machine-readable record by LC was probably the best means of standardization.

A significant step in the automation of cataloging is in development of the Ohio College Library Center, mentioned above in the section on networks. Under the direction of Kilgour, the system allows member libraries to access, search, and add to a MARC–based online bibliographic data base. When a search is successful, a command to produce a set of catalog cards can be given, and the cards arc printed in batch mode and sent to the requesting library ready to be filed. Changes may be made in the data that are displayed as the master record; the library making those changes will receive a set of cards altered to its specifications, while the master record itself remains untouched. Original cataloging may be entered into the data base by those libraries encountering unsuccessful searches, and these records may be made available to other users of the system and tagged as being locally input. The philosophy of OCLC is to attempt, within reason, to accommodate unique library cataloging features while continuing to maintain a generalized system. The network may encounter conflicting standards when many libraries begin to input original records; the resolution of this problem will be of importance for cooperative bibliographical system.

Incorporation of the Ohio College Library Center (OCLC) as a not-for-profit corporation occurred on July 6, 1967. As expressed in the Article of Incorporation, the purpose of the corporation is "to establish, maintain and operate a computerized, regional library center to serve the academic libraries of Ohio (both state and private) and designed so as to become a part of any national electronic network for bibliographical communication." The director of the Center took up his duties in Columbus in early September and spent most of the next two months consummating legal organization. System design was initiated, however, during this period, and following OCLC formal organization meetings at the end of October, system design became the main order of business. This article narrates the development of the design of a computerized regional library system in the early months of the Center's existence. As a case history, the paper contains early efforts and diagnosis; at this writing it is too early for prognosis.

The history of events leading up to the establishment of OCLC helps shed light on the Center. The Ohio College Association (OCA) was responsible for founding OCLC. The Ohio College Association is a venerable organization that came into being in 1867 as the

Association of Ohio Colleges; it changed its name to the present form in 1890. In 1867 there were a dozen charter members, including both state and private institutions; a century later, there are over sixty full and associate members. For a hundred years these Ohio institutions have been working together with effectiveness that has long since spawned mutual confidence and allowed for the stability of OCA. Perhaps the major factor behind the establishment of OCLC is this long and quiet tradition of effective cooperation among Ohio academic institutions.

MARC-Oklahoma (MARC-O) is based in the Oklahoma Department of Libraries and provides MARC tape services to users. The New England Library Information Network.is a computer-assisted center for centralized technical processing. It included initially the universities of Connecticut, Maine, Massachusetts, New Hampshire, Rhode Island and Vermont. Writing in 1970, Alan D. Ferguson states about NELINET:

> *NELIKET does not yet have its own facilities, staff, or machinery. It must be subsidized extensively even though some cataloging services can be sold to participating libraries. It is the conviction of the project's administrators that a point has been conclusively made: automated technical processing services for large networks of college, university, and research libraries can be rendered efficiently by a centralized, regional, computer-assisted center.*

These services can go far beyond cataloging and can probably include acquisitions control, the production of book-type library catalogs and serials holding lists, circulation control, and library management information systems.

The payoff in case terms will be long term. But more important, the library's capacity for service to users will be immeasurably increased and the campus library undoubtedly remain the dynamic informational core of higher educational institutions.

On the back of the title-page of some current American books partial bibliographic description is being given as the result of the program called Cataloging-in-Publication (CIP). William J. Welsh, Director of the Processing Department at the Library of Congress, describes this newly developed LC service:

Briefly expressed, the CJP entry will contain everything now on an LC printed card except for the information between the end of the title proper and the beginning of the series statement. Spelled out, the following information will be supplied: author, title, series statement, notes, subject and added entries, LC classification number, DC classification number, and LC card member. The entry will normally appear on the verso of the title page, printed in a format similar to the LC catalog card format. Entries for children's books will add annotations of the type now carried on our catalog-cards for juvenile literature. Typography of the cataloging entry will probably match that of the book.

CIP information is supplied chiefly on American trade books for major publishers. It is planned to be expanded to include additional publishers in the future. There are presently similar national systems in the Soviet Union, Colombia, Brazil and Peru. Canada is also in the process of developing such a program.

Another source for bibliographic description are the printed catalogs of the Library of Congress, especially the National Union Catalog. These catalogs consist of photographically reduced copies of Library of Congress Cards. The purpose of the printed National Union Catalog (NUC) is stated below:

> *The National Union Catalog is designed as a current and cumulative continuation of A Catalog of Books Represented by Library of Congress Printed Cards and its supplements. It represents the works cataloged by the Library of Congress and by the libraries contributing to its cooperative cataloging program during the period of its coverage. 1 addition, it includes entries for monographic publications issued in 1956 and thereafter reported by about 950 North American Libraries and not represented by LC printed cards. It constitutes a reference and research tool for a large part of the world's production of significant books as acquired and cataloged by the Library of Congress and a number of other North American libraries. For monographic works published since 1956 it Indicates at least one library where the publication is held and serves thereby, at least for these imprints, as a National Union Catalog. It serves also, by indicating the LC card number, as a tool for the ordering of LC printed cards. It is supplemented by the other parts of the Library of Congress Catalogs.*

Cataloging

If there is no Library of Congress cataloging information available for the book, then the cataloger must do original cataloging indicating the author, the title, the edition, the number of pages in the book, and any other pertinent descriptive information. All of this information is included on the catalog card as well as the call number and the subject headings. The call number consists of the classification number and the author number. The subject headings are descriptive words or phrases indicating the subject content of the book.

The first element on a catalog card is the heading or the main entry. This is usually the verified form of the author's name. The main entry may occur in four possible forms. It may be a personal author, a corporate author, a uniform title, or even a title entry. Personal authors are the most common form of main entry. A corporate entry is the entry under some corporate body such as a society, association, government, or institution which is chiefly responsible for the existence of the work. The third possibility is entry under a uniform title, as for example "Mother Goose." Finally, if none of the above may be chosen for main entry, then a work may be entered under its own title. In this last case the heading and the body are combined and hanging idention is used.

The two most common authorities are the Library of Congress Printed Catalogs and the H. W. Wilson company's Cumulative Book Index. The verifier muse take care not to be confused by these two sources. Occasionally there will be variations as to how an individual name is entered. In cases of doubt it is usually better to follow the Library of Congress practice. In addition, there are many other possible biographical dictionaries and directories which may be used for verification purposes. The other method of establishing the proper form for main entries is to use the rules given in the standard cataloging codes, of which the Anglo-American Cataloging Rules is our present one. By using rules and principles the cataloger will also have to consult bibliographical sources.

The second element on a catalog card is called the body of the card. The body consists of the title-page elements of the description. The first part of the body is the title of the book. This is followed by any necessary repetition of the author statement as it appears on the title page. The third element of the body includes the edition, the editor, the illustrator, the translator, etc. The last element of the body of the card is the imprint, consisting of the place of publication, the name of the publisher, and the date of publication, in that order. If the latest copyright date differs from the date of publication both are given. The four sections of the body of the card are consistent in that order. If any information necessary for one of the four sections does not appear on the title page but, let us say, on the page following the title page, that information will be incorporated in the body of the card.

The third part of the card is the collation, which is the cataloger's physical description of the material. It consists of three parts: the pagination, the type of illustrations, and the size. The pagination is recorded from the last numbered page of each numbering section for single volume works and the total number of volumes for multivolume works. The type of illustrations may be simply cited as "illus." with only maps receiving special indication. The size of the book is measured in regard to the height of the book in centimeters. The order of the collation is also consistent.

The fourth section of the unit card is for notes about the material. If a book is part of a series it may well have a series note at the end of the collation line. All other notes will appear as separate paragraphs below the collation. The fifth section on a catalog card is the tracing. This is a record of the necessary supplementary entries that should be produced to complete the card set. The subject headings are listed in arabic numbers and the other added entries are listed in Roman numerals.

From this description it may be observed that original cataloging is a time-consuming and hence expensive operation. Individual libraries should always avoid original cataloging if at all possible. Although the use of ISBD will simplify this to some extent, individual libraries still face the possibility of each library doing original cataloging for the same material. Centralized cataloging for a consortium can resolve this problem if a centralized office were to do all original cataloging for the members of the consortium. Just as a MARC-based center can provide existing descriptions for material on catalog cards, it could provide a common original description for material. Individual libraries might have to give up special local cataloging customs or custom cataloging but the problem of each library cataloging the same book would be solved. The problem of local or custom cataloging practices had to be resolved before NEHNET could be fully operational.

Further, individual libraries could agree to catalog originally material from specific subject or national areas and then submit such to the regional center for the use of all member libraries. Such original cataloging could include not only the descriptive cataloging but also the subject cataloging as mentioned in the following section.

Subject Cataloging

Subject cataloging deals with the assignment of classification numbers and subject headings to the individual books being cataloged. Library of Congress cataloging services include a complete Library of Congress classification call number, and Library of Congress subject headings. The Library of Congress classification and the Dewey Decimal classification are the two most common general library classification systems in this country. The subject cataloger must determine if the classification and subject headings assigned by the Library of Congress for tin individual book arc appropriate to the local library, in resource sharing the cataloger may also consider the demands of other libraries.

As the L.C. classification call number, the Dewey Decimal classification class number, and the L.C. subject headings are all on MARC tapes, a regional MARC-type center can provide any of these to a member library. A consortium may decide to use either classification system or even allow member libraries to choose whichever they prefer. All libraries in the consortium should use L.C. subject headings as other systems of subject headings, even those developed by local libraries, are not compatible with L.C. subject headings. Often L.C, classification is preferred to Dewey Decimal classification because an entire L.C. call number is given on the L.C. catalog card. Only the class number is given for D.C. users.

Library Classification

If there is no Library of Congress cataloging information available for a book being cataloged, the cataloger must assign original call numbers and subject headings to the book. Classification brings like or similar academic disciplines and their subordinates together, separating them from unlike or different disciplines. Philosophical classification attempts to create a library classification which is really a complete classification of knowledge not knowledge as it is represented in books. The Dewey Decimal classification is an example of philosophical classification. Book classification attempts to be a system based on the books themselves, not simply the knowledge represented by them. The Library of Congress classification is an example of book classification.

The codification of a classification system into numbers, letters and/or symbols is the notation. The notation is simply a process or method of representing by symbols a specific subject or subjects in a classification system. The notation is naturally a function of the classification and not the classification a function of the notation. The call number consists of the entire notation or coding device given to each particular book. This particular notation is used to locate relatively the position of a book on the shelves. The class number consists of the part of the notation resulting solely from the classification system. The book number or author number consists of the remainder of the entire notation or call number. It is normally used to create an alphabetical order within a specific subdivision of the classification on the shelf. From the latter part of the nineteenth century until the present, many general and specialized library classification schemes have been developed. The two most important schemes in English are the Dewey Decimal classification and the Library of Congress classification. Melvil Dcwey published the first edition of his system in 1876 and it has undergone many revisions and new editions. The latest edition of D.C. is the eighteenth, published in 1971. L.C. classification was developed by subject specialists at the Library of Congress to class the largest collection of material in this country. Its individual classes have been published from 1901 to the present time. L.C. uses a mixed notation consisting of letters and numbers.

Original classification using either L.C. or D.C. can create problems for individual libraries. If a library is using L.C. classification the classifier must attempt to classify originally material in a fashion like the material would have been classified at the Library of Congress. This means that the classifier must not only be familiar with the L.C. classification schedules and tables, but also with the actual application of these schedules and tables. He must compare his original class numbers with the library's shelf list of previously classified material. If a library is using the Dewey Decimal classification, the classifier may be following the D.C. numbers on L.C. cards for existing cataloged material or he may be following local autonomies within his library. In either case he must carefully consult the shelf list to determine the proper call number.

All of the copies of an individual title would receive the same L.C. call number or D.C. call number. Although both systems could exist in, consortium, a single system would be more efficient. If both systems are in use, material would have to be classified twice - once by L.C. and once by D.C. In order to have subject cataloging performed by a central agency for the entire consortium, a union shelf list must be maintained. A shelf list is a card catalog arranged by classification numbers. To classify originally a shelf list is a necessity. However, it is possible that a union shelf list could be stored in a machine readable record; in fact, the same machine readable record could also be the union catalog. This then suggests the possibility of a centralized cataloging and classification agency for a consortium.

Subject Headings

Subject headings are descriptive words or phrases designed to convey subject content of books. In 1914 the Library of Congress issued the first edition of Subject Headings Used in the Dictionary Catalogues of the Library of Congress. The present edition is the seventh and was published in 1966. L.C. subject headings, just as is the case with L.C. classification, are developed from the actual holdings of the Library of Congress. L.C. subject headings appear on L.C. printed cards. L.C. subject headings may be used either with L.C. classification or any other classification system, especially D.C. Subject headings may be simple nouns, qualified nouns, phrases, proper names, or geographic names.

Marking and Binding

The filial step in processing the book consists of marking the call number on the spine of the book mid including any necessary circulation materials in the books, such as book cards, pockets, etc. All such materials may be produced centrally. The cataloger must also determine if the book's binding is acceptable for circulation. If the binding is not acceptable the book must be sent to the bindery or given a special binding at the library. The final step in the processing of the catalog cards is to reproduce as many copies of the basic or unit card as is necessary. In a resource sharing system cards may be made for a union catalog. The copies will have separate index entries typed at the top of each card for the subject headings and the title and any other basic index or access points. Then, the card set for the book is filed in the public catalog and the shelf list.

If a centralized acquisitions unit is established for a consortium and if a centralized cataloging and classification unit is established for a consortium, then it naturally follows that a centralized processing unit could easily evolve.

Centralized processing may be defined as "those steps whereby library materials the several independent libraries, either by contract or informal agreement, are ordered, cataloged, and physically prepared for use by library patrons, these operations being performed in one location with billing, packing, and distribution to these same libraries".

Conclusion

The cataloging activities are analogous or nearly identical whether libraries perform these for themselves-or in a consortium. However, there are some points that must be reemphasized. First, cataloging and classification is often done by many libraries for the same book. Second, libraries that follow special cataloging formats or custom cataloging may introduce differences that are time-consuming to perform and expensive to pay for, often without a cost benefit rationale. Internal consistency does not necessarily mean that the catalog will be easier for the user; it may only be easier for the librarian to use. In a resource sharing system standardization of cataloging and the catalog card would be essential. In most cases this can easily be done by following Library of Congress cataloging exactly. Third, cooperating institutions may wish to agree on the use of a common classification such as the Library of Congress classification provided on Library of Congress cards. However, autonomous classification can create serious if not impossible problems for resource sharing. Users of one institution within the system should be able to access effectively the holdings of another institution with a common classification. Fourth, for all materials needing original cataloging a temporary author title file may be necessary to permit access to that material. This can relate directly to the previously suggested union file for on-order and in-process material.

In conclusion, a centralized cataloging and processing program should include the following if a resource sharing consortium is to be most effective:

1. Use of the ISBD for all consortium cataloging
2. Consortium participation in or development of a MARC-based centralized cataloging center
3. A centralized original cataloging unit
4. Use of L. C. subject headings by all member libraries
5. Consistent use of centrally of classification systems possibly, use of only L.C. classification
6. A centralized original subject cataloging unit (including classification and subject headings)
7. A union shelf list
8. A union catalog
9. A centralized processing unit

Books Keeping

As the existing shelf space in libraries becomes crowded, many libraries have developed special or separate storage libraries to warehouse little used material. The criteria for storage decisions are concerned with whether to discard a book, to microfilm it, or to store it. These decisions need to be made in regard to minimum use of the material, the cost to store it, the available space in both the library and the storage area, and the accessibility of the storage area. The minimum use of desirable books for a research library will be different than for an undergraduate library. Also the minimum use will often be different between the sciences social and physical and the humanities. The cost of storing individual material must be carefully considered. Is it worth the storage cost or should the book be discarded? Further, is there adequate space in the storage library for the material? Finally, how accessible is the storage library? Will the need for the material be reduced if the user is delayed in receiving the book? All of these factors will affect the development of criteria for storage decisions.

The problems and processes of a storage collection include the actual selection of materials for storage, the changing of existing library records, the physical moving of the materials into storage, the arranging and storage marking of the materials, the processes of retrieving materials, and the building costs of storage libraries. After criteria have been developed, the material to be stored must be selected from the library's collection. All of the records in the library's catalogs must be changed to indicate that the material is in storage. Further, the material may be given new markings for special storage shelf arrangements. Often books are stored by size to allow more compact shelving. If a large number of books arc to be moved into storage at one time, the plan for the physical move must be carefully made, including the arranging of the material in the storage library. The amount of time to receive a book from storage as well as the actual retrieval system must be readily known to library users, The distance between a storage library and the main library can often be a factor, as storage libraries are often built in areas where land is not as valuable as is the land where the main library is located. Besides the cost of the land, there are other different building costs to be considered. Although a storage library will allow greater square footage to be used, it will need to have stronger floors than a normal library building. Also, a storage library should have a lower lighting bill as the lights only need to be in use when material is being retrieved from a particular area.

The actual shelving for a storage library may make use of conventional library shelving or restricted access. Conventional library shelving and shelf placement is not necessary in a storage library. Narrow aisles may allow installation of more shelves per square foot. Further, there are various systems of mechanical or compact movable shelving systems.

The possibilities of regional storage libraries for a consortium of libraries may provide the most immediate and dramatic effects in a resource sharing system. A regional storage library used by several members of a library resource sharing network could easily relieve the high costs of building separate storage libraries. In addition, a common storage library could also act as a potential agent for exchanging material from a library that is not using it to a library that may have use of it. Such a system of storage and exchange would have to be set up very carefully, but under specific contractual arrangements could easily be done. Further, a common storage library may allow individual members to see material that may be discarded from the collection if enough copies are already in storage.

On the other hand, a more integrated single storage library, such as the Midwestern Center for Research Libraries, may be desirable. This storage center, completed in 1951, is located on the University of Chicago campus. James D. Lee describes its development and differences from the New England Deposit Library:

As joint storage became more attractive and expedient, the spectrum of participation grew broader. In 1949, ten universities cooperated to organize the Mid-west Inter-Library Center (MILC) with the primary purpose of increasing library research resources for member institutions. Participating libraries, representing universities located in eight states of the Midwest, provided supporting funds. The building, with a capacity of three million volumes, was completed in 1951; the first years were confined to the pooling and cooperative purchasing of materials, with emphasis on the deposit program. Communication with the Center by member was by teletype for some years, but was discontinued for lack of use. By 1965 deposits had reached the two million mark; the deposit program was reduced and more emphasis was placed on acquisitions. From the outset there were some functions on a national basis at the Center, such as service to all libraries irregardless of membership. Another was a serials program funded by the National Science Foundation.

In either case all the previously cited criteria for a storage library must be considered.

For a consortium storage library to be effective, its program of operation should include the following:

1. A union catalog of storage library
2. A consortium agreement on the use of priorities of stored material
3. A clearly stated policy on the amount of time to retrieve material from storage
4. A possible consortium exchange agreement for stored material.

Document Delivery Technique

The informational services of libraries include direct searches, researching questions and topics, interlibrary loans, and referrals to other libraries. First, direct searches involve the Immediate delivery of library informational services to a patron. This includes such searches as supplying simple factual answers to questions, or providing the desired document to a patron. Second, researching questions or topics includes providing a patron with a list of citations which refer to a stated question or topic; also, some libraries have: developed SDI system (Selective Dissemination of Information) based on individualized patron profiles to keep the patron aware of developments in the areas of his interest. Third, a library may supply desired documents for research purposes on the National Interlibrary Loan system developed by the American Library Association. Journal articles may be copied and sent to the library requesting the loan of the material. The patron can then receive a photocopy of the article he wishes and only has to pay the copying fee of the lending library. Monographic material can be loaned from one library to another and the patron requesting the material may use if for a stated period of time - usually two to three weeks. It is the responsibility of the patron's home library to return the material to the lending library. In this case, the home library should act as a professional referral agency. The user should be sent with specific instructions as well as potential named contacts in much the same manner that one physician might refer a patient to another physician or a lawyer might refer a client to another lawyer. The home or original librarian should follow up with both the user and the outside contact to determine if the user receive the desired information or material. If there is any potential service charge for the information or material, the home librarian should carefully alert the user of this. Patrick's study finds forty percent of her consortia sample providing this type of referral reference service.

> *Based on the literature and case study, it would appear that this service consists of members consulting each other by telephone or teletype for reference questions they cannot answer. One librarian described this service as an "interlibrary loan of ideas and answers. One procedure being considered by one of the case study consortia was to employ a reference librarian, who would be assigned to the largest library, to handle reference questions of the consortium members. One librarian's reasoning was that if he could have access In this manner to the reference collection of the larger library, he would not have to build as extensive a reference for this own library.*

Obviously a consortium may develop a more sophisticated system of interlibrary loan among members. One possible expansion would be the adoption of ALA's "Model Interlibrary Loan Code for Regional, State, Local, or Other Special Groups of Libraries". The basic differenc between this model code mid the previously cited National Interlibrary Loan Code may be observed in the following statements of purpose and scope. The purpose of the National Code is: "to make available, for research, materials not owned by a given library, in the belief that the furtherance of knowledge is in the general interest. Interlibrary loan service supplements a library's resources by making available, for the use of an individual, materials from other libraries not owned by the borrowing library. The purpose and scope of the Model Code obviously broadens inter-library loan to include non-research materials. The Model Code states:

> *Since it is increasingly evident that it is impossible for any one library to be self-sufficient, and in the belief that the furtherance of knowledge is in the general interest, interlibrary borrowing and lending is regarded by the libraries subscribing to this agreement as essential to library service.*

An immediate advantage of expanded interlibrary loan services is cited by Patrick:

> *Judging from the case studies, the new interlibrary loan services means that services have been expanded beyond the limits set in the ALA code to include undergraduate as well as graduate (or serious) students and faculty. Another way in which interlibrary loan has been expanded is to arrange for the loaning of materials in bulk, to support seminars, tutorials or research projects in areas outside a college's regular curriculum. This imaginative use of resources may have existed before, but it has been facilitated by the consortium framework.*

Bibliographic Service

Once bibliographic access has been provided so that the locations of books are known and after interlibrary loan services have been expanded to include more categories of users, if the user does not borrow the book in person, then arrangements are needed to provide physical access to the book. Of the 125 consortia, 35% provided delivery service. Various methods of providing transportation were encountered in the case studies. One consortium instituted a study to examine alternatives of moving library materials between libraries. Alternatives ranged from helicopter service to United Parcel Service. One of the observations was that the major delay is within the libraries, not between them.

As with all the possible cooperative activities, a solution suitable for one consortium may be unsatisfactory to another. One consortium concluded that the U. S. Mail was the most economical method for them because of the low volume of materials moving between libraries; another felt that the rapidity of delivery service more than compensated for the slightly higher expense. In one consortium, one of the reasons for having a truck delivery system was that several of the members who were not on a direct mailing route found the mailing service too slow. One somewhat unique solution was to rotate the responsibility for providing transportation among the members, once every 5 weeks. The type of transportation was decided by each member and ranged from a student's car to a university-owned panel truck to a taxicab. The director reported that for 1 year, for 4, 000 transactions (which he felt was a relatively small number), the unit cost was 50C per volume transferred.

The Selective Dissemination of Information (SDI) service provides for subscribing state agencies and libraries a quick, personalized alerting service to new books in the specific subject areas of their direct interest and responsibility. Subject profiles of Dcwey and/or L.C. classification numbers are first developed by a reference librarian. These profiles are "fed" to the computer. The computer then searches each weekly MARC tape and selects MARC records which fall within the profiles and prints out a notice of bibliographic information on that new book. Each participating state agency or library receives a weekly printout of complete bibliographic information on new books in their subject fields of interest.

In order to use any library, the patron must be aware of the potential documental citations within the library. The user must be aware of and able to use or receive assistance in use of the library's public records. The library's public records include the individual library's card catalog. This record should demonstrate to the user the actual monographic holdings of other libraries; the user should be aware of these. Further, the user should consider using the standard bibliographies and indexes of monographic and periodical literature. After a user has discerned the existence of potential desired bibliographic sources, he must determine the availability of these sources. The items listed in the card catalog should be available as part of the library's holdings; so should any items in the library's periodical or serial holdings. Union catalogs, bibliographies, and indexes all will provide potential sources which may be included in the individual library's holdings or may need to be ordered on Interlibrary Loan.

Further, libraries should assist their users in using other libraries. It must be explained what other libraries' circulation rules are, and where and how far the other libraries are.

Perhaps the ideal delivery of library services would allow a user to be advised whether a library in the area has the desired material or not. This would allow the user to determine whether to order the material on Inter-library Loan, use some sort of regional cooperative delivery service, or go to the other library himself. This would further and perhaps more importantly imply that there need be a common library card and borrowing provisions for all area, or regional, or even national libraries. This sense of delivery of services would imply basic concepts of the resource sharing of libraries. Reciprocal borrowing privileges are certainly an inducement for the organization of a library consortium. Patrick lists three advantages to the user of libraries in a consortium:

Reciprocity was of special benefit to commuting students, who are now permitted to use libraries closer to their homes. Another benefit is that it enables junior college students to become acquainted with the facilities of colleges or universities they may be considering for further study. Also, in some cases a user can obtain a book he needs more quickly if he goes directly to the lending' library than if he were to wait for the material to be conveyed via interlibrary loan.

In a súmmary, the delivery of services by resource sharing has been one of the oldest cooperative activities of American libraries. This may be seen through the practice of interlibrary loans. With the development of a union catalog for a consortium, some of the costs of interlibrary loans may be reduced and limited to the libraries within the consortium. It is also possible to use common delivery methods such as trucks going from one library to another in an area. Furthermore, the potential of telecoping can provide another mechanism of transferring material from one library to another.

1. A consortium interlibrary loan system.
2. A possible consortium SDI system.
3. A consortium teletype network.
4. A union catalog.
5. A consortium delivery system.

5

LIBRARY RESOURCE SHARING THROUGH NETWORKING

When will the technology be capable of supporting effective library resource sharing? The answer is now; and network resource sharing is already an accomplished fact of life. To paraphrase one of the key findings of the recent National Academy of Sciences sponsored study into libraries and information technology, the primary bar to development of automated library networks is no longer a technology feasibility problem. Rather it is the combination of institutional, organizational, human related and economic value system problems. Therefore it is our aim here to demonstrate that readily available information storage, information processing, and information transfer technology can facilitate the sharing of library resources.

A Basic Network Model

Before moving into information technology, it may be worthwhile to take a brief look at how information flows in a network while bibliographic to networks may assume a variety of sizes and configurations, they usually exhibit three basic classes of functions:

1. Information storage.
2. Information processing and control, and
3. Information transfer.

The general relationship among these functions is as in Fig 5.1.

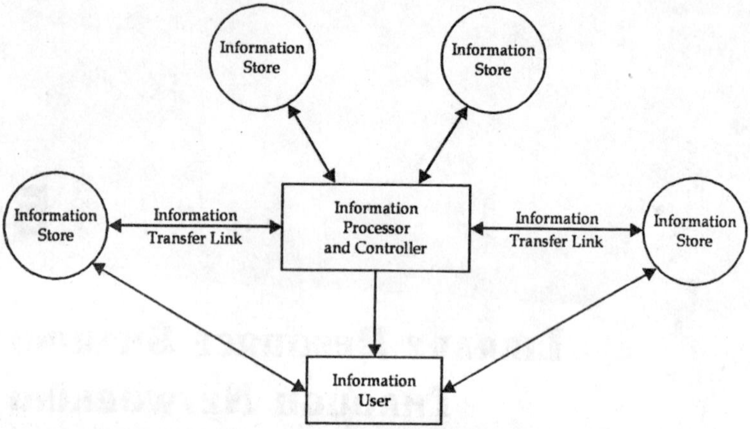

Figure 5.1

Information may be stored in various forms. It may be extracted from the stores and processed in various ways. It may then be transferred back to the original store or to various other stores. Information users can extract information directly from an information store or indirectly via information processor and controller node. There is no theoretical limit to the number of stores or processors. In a library network, the basic form of storage (or at least the original input form to the system). Is the printed document, and the primary storage facility is the library. The user may be considered an information network himself, as he is both an information processor and an information store. He can create information, extract information, intellectually process it, and store it for later use. He may even return his stored and processed information to the library in the form of a new document.

Modern technology can now provide us with many ways in which library networks can store, process, and transfer information to facilitate resource sharing economically, effectively, and on a scale that would be near impossible with traditional manual operations.

How to Store Information

Most living things possess the ability to store and retrieve information. Man, however, has expanded significantly his ability to store and retrieve information through the development and application of various forms of technology. This ability to artificially store information resources for future retrieval and utilization is the raison d'etre of the library. Without the capacity for relatively large scale information storage and retrieval, the library network cannot function effectively.

There is a wide range of media which can be used to store information, Camras in his review of the subject identified over 20 potential information storage media with different storage densities, storage capacities, and access speeds. Among these are:

1. **Graphic: Storage Techniques (Paper)**
   - Typed page
   - Book page
   - Halftone picture
   - Snapshot photo
2. **Graphic Storage Techniques (Non-Paper)**
   - 35mm color slide
   - Microfilm
   - Videotape
3. **Sound Storage Techniques**
   - Phonodisks
   - Sound Tape
4. **Digital Storage Techniques**
   - Computer data register and logic
   - Magnetic core memory
   - Magnetic drum
   - Punched cards
   - Thin film memory
   - Magnetic disk file
   - Computer tape
5. **Biological Storage Techniques**
   - Human brain and nervous system
   - Genetic

Fig 5.2 presents Camras' ranking of a number of these storage systems according to a figure of merit (known as "CDS Rating") which considers storage Capacity, storage. Density and Speed of access. Although several years old now, Camras' comparison is still valid and interesting.

In the discussion below, we would like to review some developments in the two areas of storage technology that most lend themselves to the library network environment, digital storage technology and graphic storage technology.

The distinctions between digital and graphic storage are essentially the form in which the information is stored. Graphic information may be stored in the form of books, catalog cards, photographs, microfilm, and videotape. Digital information generally includes any coded representation which can be processed by machines without first requiring transformation to machine language.

Computer Storage

Digital storage normally refers to a form of machine readable information storage which will allow the information to be processed by computer. Libraries have begun to store more and more of their information (particularly cataloging data) in digital form to allow for rapid and efficient processing by computer. As Mathews and Brown [3] point out, a digitally stored catalog has many advantages over the common card catalog, the book catalog and the microform catalog. These major advantages include:

1. Speed in searching
2. Ease of updating
3. Ease of restructuring to facilitate different search strategies
4. Ease of conversion to other media, such as microform (via computer output microfilm) or paper (via a high speed printer)
5. Ease of rapid duplication of additional machine readable copies for dissemination to other libraries (such as with the Library of Congress MARC [Machine Readable Catalog] magnetic tapes)
6. Ease of merging two or more machine readable catalogs to produce a union catalog.

These advantages (despite the attendant disadvantage of high input cost) definitely justify serious consideration of digital storage for library network applications.

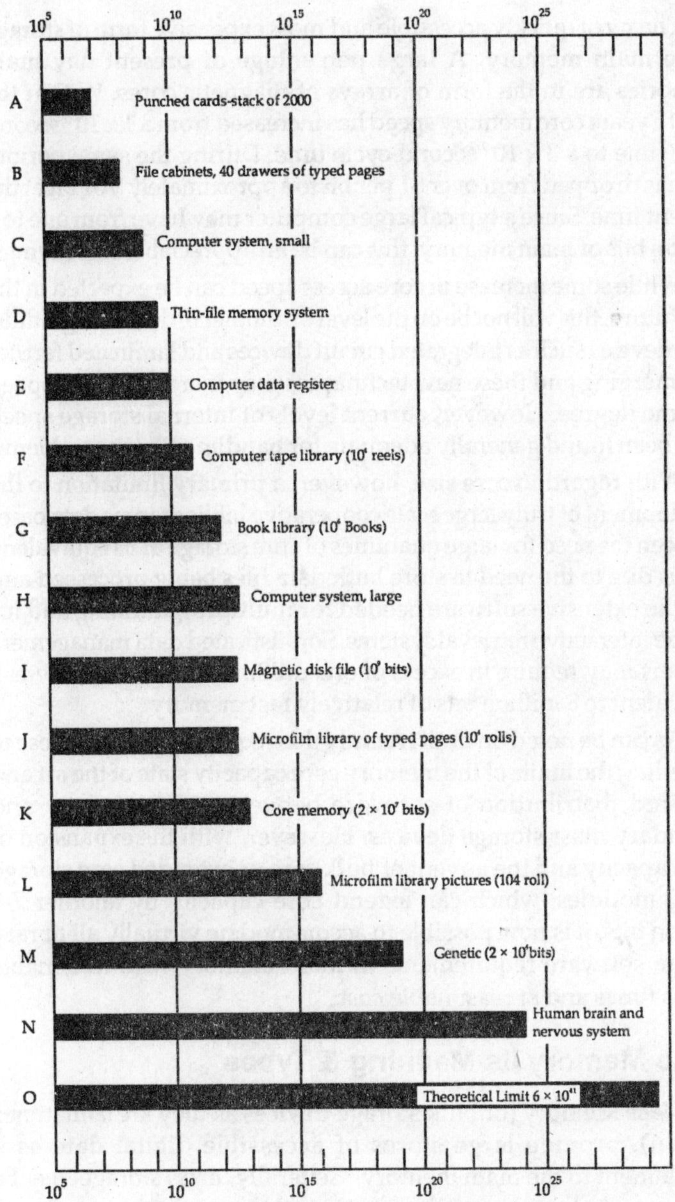

Figure 5.2. CDS Rating, total bits × bits/cm³ × bits/sec.

Basic Memory

The most quickly accessible and most expensive form of storage is the main memory. A large percentage of present day main memories are in the form of arrays of magnetic cores. Within the past 15 years core memory speed has increased from a 1×10^{-5} second cycle time to a 3×10^{-7} second cycle time. During the same period, cost has dropped from over $1 per bit to approximately $ 01 bit at the present time. Since a typical large computer may have from one to 8 million bits of main memory, this can be an appreciable cost savings.

While some increase in core access speed can be expected in the near future, this will not be on the level of another order of magnitude. New devices such as integrated circuit devices and laminated ferrites are emerging and these new techniques may increase access speed to some degree. However, current levels of internal storage speed have been found generally adequate for handling library problems.

With regard to core size, however, a primary limitation to the development of truly large scale cooperative bibliographic data bases has been the need for large quantities of core storage of its equivalent. This is due to the need to store both data files being processed and also the extensive software needed for multiprogramming and for on-line interactive retrieval systems. Sophisticated data management systems may require in excess of one million characters (or bytes), equivalent to 8 million bits of relatively fast memory.

As can be noted on until recently this requirement came close to exceeding the limits of the memory core capacity state of the art and required distribution of software between main memory and secondary mass storage devices. However, with the expansion of core capacity and the advent of bulk core or extended core storage (ECS) modules, which can extend core capacity by another 7-8 million bits, it is now possible to accommodate virtually all library system software requirements in main memory with reasonable access times and at reasonable cost.

Mass Memory its Meaning & Types

Mass Memory (or bulk storage devices as they are sometimes known), provide large stores of accessible digital data as a supplement to the main memory. Generally, mass storage may be considered to be either random on these devices must be transferred to the main core memory before it can be processed. Of particular

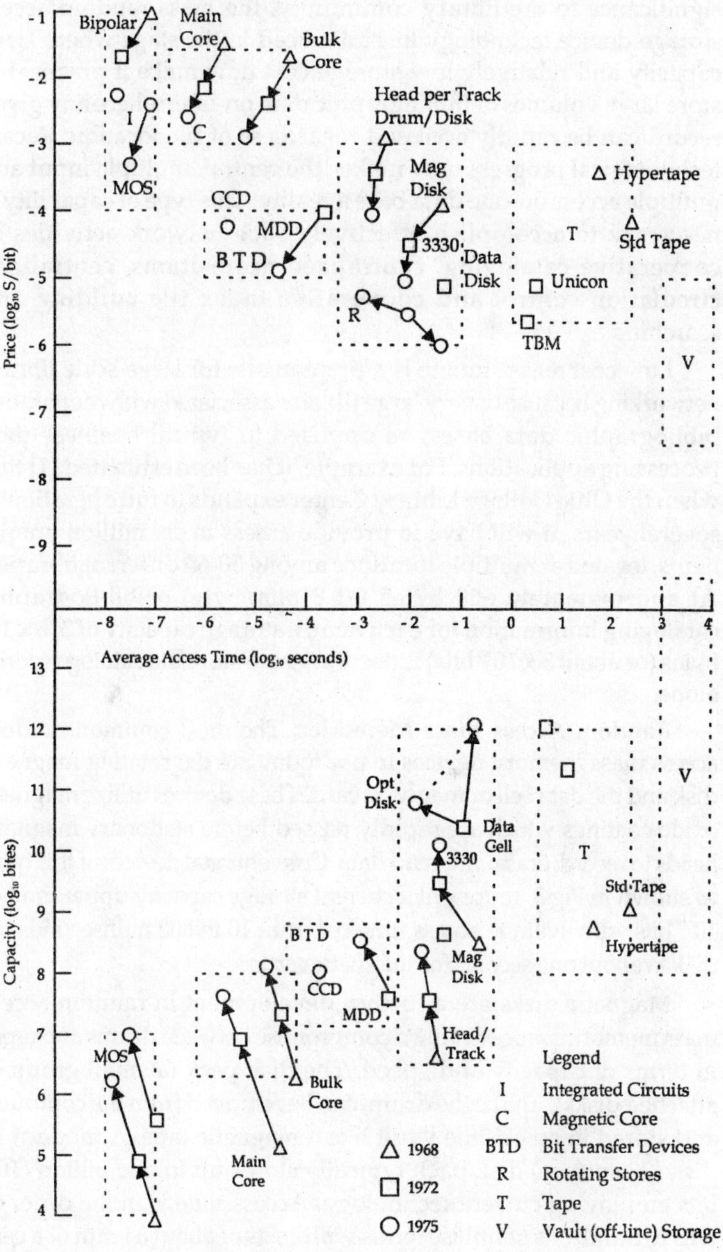

Figure 5.3. Computerize Storage

significance to the library community, the mass random access storage device technology has advanced to the stage where large capacity and relatively low storage cost now make it practical to store large volumes of bibliographic data on-line, where any given record can be rapidly accessed regardless of file location. Recent technological progress now makes the central, multiple input and multiple access on-line data base a reality. This type of capability is necessary to accomplish effectively such network activities as cooperative cataloging, centralized acquisitions, centralized circulation control and cooperative index file building and searching.

Low cost mass storage is a prerequisite for large-scale library networking because of very large file size associated with cooperative bibliographic data bases; as opposed to typical business data processing applications. For example, it has been estimated [1] that when the Ohio College Library Center expands to full operation in several years, it will have lo provide access to six million unique items, located at multiple locations among 50-60 different libraries. At approximately 600 bytes (at 8 bits/byte) of bibliographic cataloging information for each item, a storage capacity of 3.6×10^9 bytes (or about 3×10^{10} bits) is needed just to store the catalog records alone.

Random Access Mass Memories: The most common random access mass memory devices in use today are the rotating magnetic disk and the data cell or magnetic card. These devices utilize magnetic oxide coatings which are rapidly passed before stationary magnetic heads to record, erase, and read data. Conventional devices of this type, as shown in Fig.3, represent a current storage capacity upper limit of 10^{10} bits with average access times of from 10 to 600 milliseconds for disk to about one second for magnetic cards.

Magnetic disks are a further development in random access mass memories representing a compromise between drums and tapes in terms of capacity and speed. The disk pack (a small group of attached disks), unlike the drum, can be removed from the computer and stored in an off-line vault like a magnetic tape. A modern 10 disk (20 surface) disk pack typically stores up to one billion (10^9) bits employing current technology. Access time is in the order of tens to hundreds of milliseconds with costs of about a tenth of a cent per bit or less.

Magnetic cards (such as the IBM Data Cell system), though still in use in some bibliographic operations, are losing popularity because of their relatively slow access speeds. Their major advantage is their ability to store large quantities of data at a relatively small cost per storage bit. A typical magnetic card system can store 4×10^8 characters or bytes of data (equivalent to 3. 2 billion bits) at a cost of roughly 1/1000 of a cent per bit. However, access time is rather poor, approaching one second, which is normally not acceptable for most on-line applications,

Advanced Random Access Mass Memory Technology: It has been predicted that several significant advances in mass memory technology can be anticipated. Dr. William Shockley, inventor of the transistor, recently stated: "It is in the area of computer memory that man's greatest inventions will likely come. Machine memory will be increased a billion-fold, not a million-fold over its present level."

Several emerging areas of mass storage technology, now in the experimental or developmental stages, hold the promise of improving access time and of extending storage capacity at least two orders of magnitude to 12 or 13 bits without appreciable increase in cost. These developments may encourage library resource sharing by enabling larger numbers of libraries to pool data economically while ensuring rapid retrieval access.

Magnetic Memory Technique

The magnetic bubble memory, a major technique being developed by Bell Telephone Laboratories and others, bears close watching. This experimental memory, also known as the Bit Transfer Device (BTD) and the Magnetic Domain Device (MDD), may provide random access devices in the billion bit range with a reduction in access time of at least two orders of magnitude. This feat is accomplished by eliminating mechanical rotational and read head movement. Another experimental form of BTD is the Charge Coupled Device (CCD) which uses Metal Oxide Semiconductors (MDS).

Laser optical recording on magnetic and amorphous semiconductor media can increase storage density to the point where the trillion bit random access disk store may be commercially available within the next two years. As evidence of the advancing pace of mass memory technology, a potentially significant breakthrough was announced recently. This is the 10 trillion (10^{13}) bit optical laser memory. The performance characteristics and price of this new development were reported as "staggering" and they represent significant potential for library system applications. This random access optical mass memory provides access rates of only 20 nanoseconds (20×10^{-9}) at a cost of about 2×10^{-5}c per bit. That means that this memory is capable of storing a library of 2.5 million books a cost of about $ 8 per book. With a device such as this it now becomes possible to store the equivalent of all available Library of Congress catalog card data on a single random access device. The company that has announced this new memory (Laser Computer Corpo-ration) is also planning to develop an atomic lattice memory with the mind-boggling storage capacity of 10^{40} bits.

Serial Access (Magnetic Tape) Mass Memories: Although it was the first form of digital computer storage, magnetic tape is rapidly losing favor as a mass storage medium. As random access drums and disks become larger and cheaper, the relatively slow access speed of the tape, engendered by its serial search mode, becomes more of a problem. (Magnetic tape, however, is gaining in popularity as a bibliographic information dissemination device to be discussed later in this paper). The advantage of magnetic tape is that it is the least expensive form of mass storage (about 5/100 of a cent per bit, or .015c per 30 bit word). Magnetic tapes, because of their compact size, are as easy to store as books.

A standard magnetic tape is capable of storing over one million English language words. However, to pass the entire tape from beginning to end in order to access a particular piece of information, may require as much as five minutes. This delay may be intolerable under certain circumstances despite the relatively low storage cost of magnetic tape.

Associative Memories

Content addressable or associative memory systems have been under; investigation since 1955. Of interest to the library community is the capability of the associative memory to identify and correlate information items on the basis of their content, not only by their name or position.

Although relatively small scale associative memories have been constructed and are operational evidence today that indicates that associative memory arrays with a capacity of a billion bits will be available within the next five to ten years.

Graphic Storage Technology

The most common form of graphic storage device, and, in fact, the most common information storage device, in current use is the one most common to libraries; the print on paper (or hard copy) medium exemplified by the book. Although the thrust of this paper is directed at nonbook media, there are several technological comments which can be made about the book, as contrasted with other technology based information storage systems. This contrast was made by Bruno W. Augenstern, vice president of the RAND Corporation. The major advantages of the book as a information storage and dissemination medium are:

1. The match to the human scale (the hand and eye particularly).
2. Portability— no artificial power needs or requirement for power outlets (who will ever use an electronic visual information device in places like the bathroom and the beach?).
3. Indefinite storage life without degradation.
4. Relative permanence of information, compared to risks inherent in electronic devices where sheer inadvertence can destroy the information.
5. Ability to function as an informative transmission and storage device over an extremely wide range of environments.

Microform Storage Technology

At this point in time, the digital storage of full text documents is still not economically feasible. Therefore, as an alternative to paper hard copy document storage, increasing attention has been directed at microforms as both an information storage and transfer medium. In fact there is a distinct trend towards hybrid systems which couple the information manipulation capabilities of the computer with the full text storage qualities of microforms. Two examples are the computer driven microform information retrieval systems and computer output microfilm better known by its initials, COM.

Microform as a storage and transfer medium offers a number of distinct advantages which could be exploited in library network applications:

1. Compact storage of information (with a storage density of about 10^8 bits/CM^3 compared to $1O^3$ bits/CM^3 for a magnetic disk and 10^4 bits/CM^3
2. High fidelity recording of both text and images in black and white and color
3. Economical and facile replication (1/10c per page or less for microform to microform replication)
4. Ease of dissemination and transport (an entire microfiche document can be mailed in a single letter-size envelope for 8c first class postage)

Microforms Types & Principal

1. Roll microfilm : The medium first used in modern microfilming applications. The microimages lie on a roll of film, either in cine orientation (arranged like the frames on a roll of motion picture film, with the horizontal lines of the microimages perpendicular to the edge of the film) or in comic strip or orientation (arranged like the frames of a comic strip, with the horizontal lines of the microimages parallel to the edge of the film). Both perforated and unperforated film is used; the most common film widths are 16mm and 35mm, but 70mm and 105mm film are desirable in certain situations.

2. Cartridges: A convenient way of handling roll microfilm. Film is packed in a cartridge, in much the same way as film is packed for cartridge-type amateur cameras. The cartridge is easily placed on the reader; film advance and rewind are usually motorized.

3. Aperture cards: Single microfilm frames mounted in 3 1/4 x 7 3/8" cards. The film fits into a window cut in the card. Cards can carry printed legends identifying the frames and can also be coded with Hollerith punches for machine sorting, since they have the same overall size as Standard EDP cards.

4. Film cards: Cards containing one or more pockets to hold strips of microfilm. The strips are removed from the pockets and placed in the reader for viewing.

5. Microfiche: A group of microfilm frames arranged in a rectangular pattern on a piece of film. The fiche are manually inserted into the reader and moved until the desired microimage is projected onto the screen. Horizontal and vertical coordinates of the projected item are often indicated by a pointer moving across a grid card or by built in scales.

6. Microprint: Rows of microimages on an opaque paper card. Except for its opacity, it resembles microfiche. The opacity, however, prevents use with standard microfiche readers. Special readers are available.

What has traditionally been a drawback in the use of microforms, the lack of low cost high quality viewing equipment, may be eliminated as the result of a recently announced breakthrough. A completely new technique, under development by Dr. Adnan Waly, employs a "fly's eye" system of 3500 minute spherical lenses which break down a page into a matrix pattern, requiring a projecting distance of less than an inch.

This development has tremendous potential impact on the library community. Dr. Waly has estimated that with this system, a 625-page book can be reproduced on microfilm for less than $25.

Microform in Network Application

In an information exchange network context, perhaps the greatest sponsor of microform has been the Federal Government. In fact, much of the recent popularity of microforms (particularly microfiche) is the result of a new approach to libraries by the Government, that of converting the library from an information circulation to an information distribution agency with microfiche serving as the storage and disseminator medium. Federal agencies such as the Office of Education's ERIC, the Defense Documentation Center, the National Technical Information Service, NASA, and the AEG have all fostered the network concept by making widespread distribution (at no charge or at a low fee) of no-return technical documents on microfiche through the United States.

This widespread distribution of entire microfiche document collections, with access facilitated through abstracting and indexing journals sponsored by the distribution agency, has fostered a national network of satellite libraries which provide users in all parts of the country with rapid access to technical reports which would have been impossible without low cost microforms. As a spokesman of the AEC stated. "This medium (microfiche) fills a critical need in that it makes possible circulation of information which should be disseminated but which has no other practical means of issuance."

An interesting commentary on the relative costs of the paper hardcopy form of storage vs. the microform is the fact that the Defense Documentation Center will provide a microfiche copy of a technical report at no charge, but imposes a $3 service charge on the hard copy version of the same document.

Videotape Technology

A graphics storage medium of increasing interest to the library community is the videotape. Videotape stores high-resolution television images on magnetic tape instead of optical images on film as with microforms. As with microfilms, videotape can be used in conjunction with a computer to provide an automated retrieval system.

Videotape systems can store 8½" x 11" pages at a density of about 36 frames per foot of 2" wide tape and 5½" to 8½" pages at a density of 72 frames per foot, including the digitally encoded address for each page. Viewing stations are television monitors, which can be linked to computer terminals on-line search and retrieval.

As a full text storage medium, videotape is still beyond the budget range of most libraries. However, as Libraries begin to consider on-line storage of full text, videotape should be considered as an alternative to digital storage. Comparative studies [19] have shown that for large volume on-line storage of up to 40 million pages of text, videotape systems are cost-competitive with digital disk storage.

Working of Information Technology

As our simplified information network model in Fig 5.1 shows, a network requires a node which both processes and manipulates information stored within the network and also provides both the operators and users of the network with a means of controlling and accessing that information. In the context of the modern information network, this processing and control function quite often entails the use of a computer. Because of its ability to keep track of and manipulate large volumes of data at extremely high speed, the computer is ideally suited to this task.

In a library network environment, we find that the data processing demands placed upon the computer may be somewhat different than those normally encountered in business or scientific applications.

Computer Hardware

With the advent of larger and faster main and mass memory devices (as discussed above), providing on-line access to huge bibliographic databases is now within the realm of economic feasibility. Similarly, advances in computer construction, such as large scale integration and advances in computer control such as multiprogramming, multiprocessing, and virtual memory have significantly reduced the cost of computer power to the point where computer processing costs are less of a problem in information processing. It has been predicted that this trend will continue.

Such features as timesharing capability, which facilitates multiple use of a data base, and the so called intelligent terminal — a terminal equipped with certain logical and processing capabilities — all contribute to dramatic reductions in processing costs. As a result, we have been able to achieve an improved price-performance ratio which brings the computer within the grasp of the many in the library community. For example, in 1959 on second generation equipment, it cost approximately $5 to process a million instructions.

The National Academy of Sciences study on libraries and information technology £p has identified the trend toward minicomputers as having great significance to libraries. Coupled with intelligent terminals, the minicomputer may foster networks built upon the concept of "distributed intelligence" [20] whereby low cost small local files may be effectively interfaced with larger central databases and computers. The decreasing cost and increasing power of minicomputers is impressive. Their price-performance index has been improving at a rate of about 50% per year since their introduction in 1963. This trend is expected lo continue through 1975 at least, as semiconductor logic and memory technology continues to evolve.

It is interesting to note that when one begins to distribute information processing functions throughout a network, such as in the case of a minicomputer network, the computers are required to

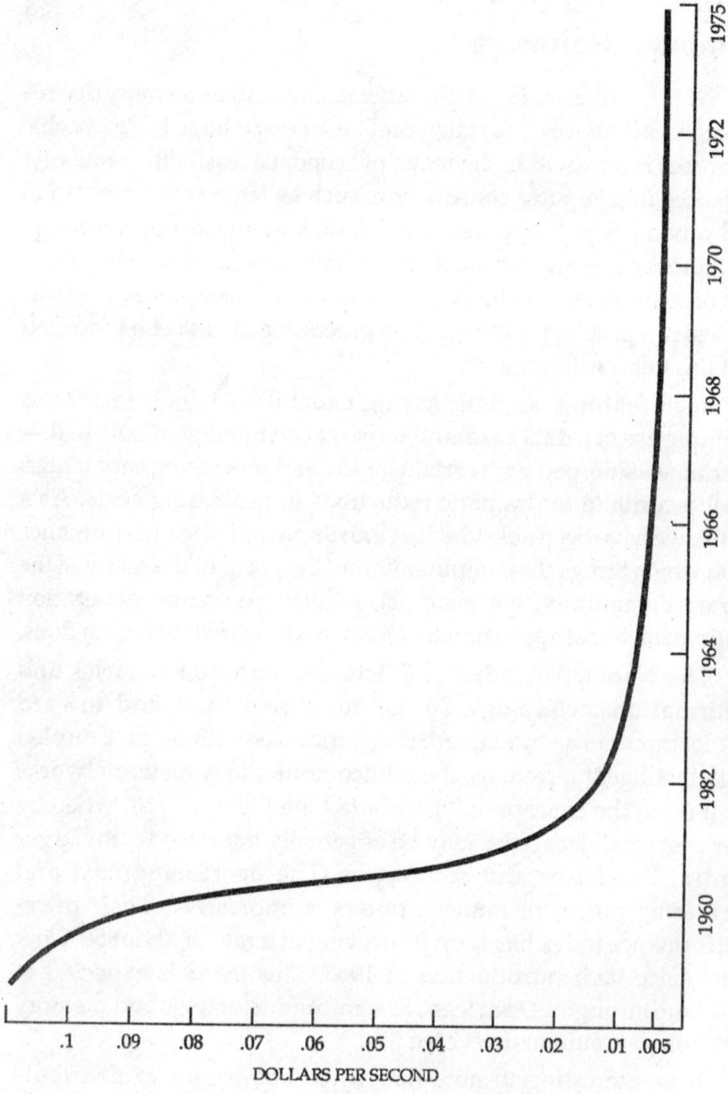

Figure 5.4. Reduction in computation cost for a computer with 10,000 operations.second capability

perform many communi-cations functions such as polling and switching. It therefore becomes difficult to separate information processing functions from information transfer functions, which is perhaps a sign of a true network relationship.

Computer Software

The area of computer programs or software is where some of both the greatest information technology problems and the moat fertile areas for real progress can be found. For the computer hardware to perform its function properly, the software systems must fully exploit its technical capabilities. However, in an evaluation of current software technology [22] Auerbach's analysts found that a definite gap exists between hardware and software developments. To fill this gap in the area of document storage and retrieval, a whole new class of applications programs, known as Information Storage and Retrieval Software, has developed over the past seven or eight years. This is true despite the fact that the "National Academy of Sciences' (NAS) report on Libraries and Information Technology found this area of software technology still in an "embryonic state."

Information storage and retrieval or data management software systems as they are also called can be characterized as performing several basic functions on the large files (or data bases) normally found in the library environment.

1. File creation
2. File maintenance (or management)
3. File manipulation
4. File searching and retrieval

These systems may operate in cither batch or on-line mode, may be full text of fixed vocabulary and normally exhibit a wide range of capabilities file structures, retrieval characteristics, and search strategies. However, there are still (and always will be) particular cases where a software package is unsatisfactory and only a custom made set of programs will do the job. As in'this area of software technology develops, librarians are finding that they can select from an ever increasing variety of "off the shelf software systems with a variety of capabilities, characteristics, and price tags.

Similarly, original software created for such networks as OCLC or SUNY may also be applicable to the needs of newly emerging library cooperatives. The administrators of any planned library cooperatives might do well to look into the possibility of obtaining software from a successful network such as OCLC. Aside from the potential savings of obtaining a proven product specifically designed for network applications, use of the same software by two or more networks will provide for a greater degree of compatibility should it ever be decided to link the systems together.

Data Change: A Process

A critical and necessary function of a library network is the transfer of bibliographic information between information stores or component libraries and between libraries and system users. When one begins to consider computer based network activity, one must also determine whether the data communications technology is capable of supporting the required information transfer functions at the various levels, ranging from transferring bulk information between central information storage nodes to providing information users with individual access to specialized data bases. As the NAS study of library technology stated.

This question of the economic feasibility of applying telecommunications technology to library networks was also addressed by the Conference on Interlibrary Communications and Information Networks which was jointly sponsored by the American Library Association and the United States Office of Education This group found that existing commercial telecommunications services were already available to accommodate most of the spectrum of communications requirements of a library network at reasonable cost.

The finding that the existing communications networks are technologically able to satisfy library network needs is not new. Ten years ago, at a conference on library automation it was stated that communications technology was not a limiting factor in interlibrary communication, but instead, the degree of telecommunication was a function of balancing benefits of geographical extension against costs. Communications networks have for some time now been capable of effectively transmitting digitally encoded messages and facsimile images over long distance. The real problem has been that of libraries finding the means to use this available capability effectively and economically.

The discussion below examines the current capability of commercially available telecommunications services.

Telecommunication Cost

As a critical consideration in determining the feasibility of a telecommunications based library network is usually cost, a general introduction of telecommunications cost parameters should be of some value before discussing the technological question.

As Dittberner points out, telecommunications costs are a function of three basic parameters

1. Distance
2. Amount of usage
3. Channel capacity (or bandwidth)

Transmission distance is a basic rate parameter used in calculating telecommunications costs. Existing rate structures are such that total cost increases with distance while cost per transmission unit either increases or remains constant with increasing distance.

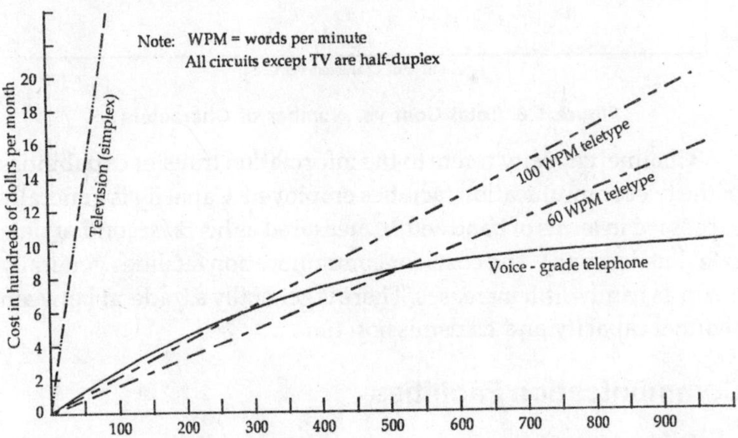

Figure 5.5. Comparison of wide band and narrow band transmission costs.

Amount of usage has a direct effect on cost. Generally, charges for telecommunications services are directly related to the length of time the service is in use. This is particularly true for message rate usage (such as with the switched dialup telephone network) where many users employ the same telephone plant. There are also flat rate programs whereby a user pays a flat fee for a certain level of telecommunications service using either dedicated or shared facilities. This type of service is also really dependent on amount of usage as the decision to employ the flat rate structure is economic, based on an estimated minimum use rate. If you fall far below the minimum rate, your cost per unit of time utilized will increase.

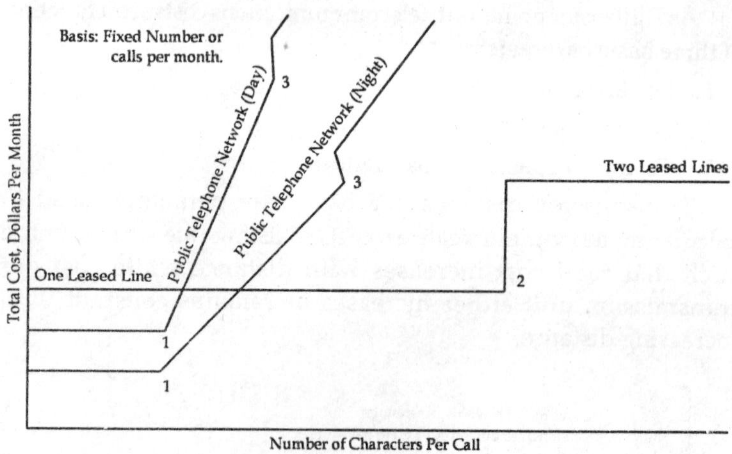

Figure 5.6. Total Cost vs. Number of Characters

Channel capacity refers to the information transfer capabilities of the telecommunication facilities employed. Capacity is generally expressed in terms of bandwidth, measured as hertz/second or data rate (bits/second). The costs for communication facilities generally go up as bandwidth increases. There is generally a tradeoff between channel capacity and transmission time.

Communication Facilities

In the United States, communications facilities can only be provided under federal authorization or by state governments. Those companies authorized to provide communications facilities are referred to as communications common carriers. The authorizations by which they are permitted to function are called tariffs; they define the acceptable operating environment such as accounting procedures, the specific geographical area of operation, and the types and costs of the offered communication facilities and services.

The major U. S. communication common carriers can be divided into five main categories:

1. Bell System companies
2. Independent telephone companies
3. Western Union Telegraph
4. Specialized common carriers
5. Communications Satellite Corporation

Of these, the first two groups, Bell System and independent telephone companies, generally provide dial telephone service for voice transmission– the stereotype of a telephone company. These organizations also offer private line facilities and certain types of terminal equipment. Western Union Telegraph and specialized common carriers provide a form of communication facilities and services primarily for data transmission. They represent communication common carriers that emphasize data or information communications; they do offer alternate voice communica-tions facilities and services.

Special Communication Services

In 1971, the FCC issued a ruling on the definition of a communications common carrier. This statement permits the formation and operation of specialized communications common carriers and allows an organization that meets basic technical and financial qualifications to request and obtain communications common carrier status. These organizations can then market communications facilities and services that are competitive with the traditional communications common carriers. Like the traditional common carriers, these new carriers must operate under tariffs.

Although a number of organizations have filed applications with the Federal Communications Commission requesting communications common carrier status, only two have been authorized to proceed with building their communications network: Microwave Communications Incorporated and Data Transmission Company.

At this time the new communications common carriers are in a formative stage. Rather than providing a broad spectrum of communications facilities and services, they have elected to market only certain types of communications facilities and services. This characteristic of specialization led to the nomenclature "specialized common carriers."

As data communications appears a prime area of interest for the specialized common carriers, library networks should definitely evaluate these organizations as potential telecommunications vehicles. It is possible that the increased competition generated by these new carriers may result in decreased library network communication costs.

Types of Facilities

Communications facilities offered by the common carriers can be broken into two classes: switched and fixed. While both categories are part of the same general communication network, the distinction is based on the manner of implementation.

1. **Switched facility:** a temporary communications connection that is available on a demand basis to one of a number of locations. It is charged on a distance time-available basis.
2. **Fixed facility:** a permanent communications connection that is provided on a scheduled, preordered basis to one or more selected locations. It is charged on a distance basis.

A switched facility generally has the system advantages associated with flexibility of time, duration, and location of connection but typically has the system disadvantage of unknown transmission characteristics. Switched facilities have virtually infinite backup capability.

A fixed facility generally has the system advantage of known transmission characteristics but the system disadvantage associated with a rigid configuration of connection. It is directly dependent on the maintenance responsiveness of personnel from one or more communica-tions common carriers for backup capability.

Data Communications Facilities and Services

The term data communications, as commonly defined refers to the transmission and receipt of alphanumeric characters over common carrier or privately owned transmission facilities. Data originates or terminates at terminal devices such as teletypewriters, cathode-ray tube (CRT) alphanumeric display consoles, digital plotters, line and page printers, punched paper tape terminals, magnetic tape units, and punched card terminals. Data transmission facilities link such terminals to remote computers or to switching centers and also link computers to each other. Record communications between terminals, as provided by the TWX and Telex teletypewriter exchanges, are also included within our definition of data communications.

The transmission and reception of data is accomplished through the following media. These facilities may operate alone or may be used together.

1. The public switched telephone network transmits digital data. It is operated by Bell System companies and the independent telephone companies.
2. The public switched telegraph network provides two-way connections between low-speed terminals. It is operated by Western Union Telegraph Company.
3. Leased private wire service provides the user with exclusive use of a communications line.
4. Privately owned microwave radio systems provide high-capacity transmission capability to users with high traffic rate.

The need for data communications results mainly from the development of computer systems in which computer terminals are placed at considerable distances from the computer itself or in which data interchange between two or more remotely located computers is desired. As data communications is a key to effective library resource sharing, the discussion below will present a number of considerations in this area.

Library Resource Sharing Cover the Area

Channel Capacity: Each of the three classes of data communications facilities, narrowband, voiceband, and wideband, has different channel capacities. The bandwidth of each type of facility is a measure of its signal carrying capacity in hertz (one hertz = one cycle per second). Therefore, in general, the broader the band, the greater the signal transmission rate (usually expressed in bits per second). Examples of typical data rate requirements are:

1. Data rate of user presenting a query to a search system -100 bits/second
2. Data rate of system reply to query-1000 bits/second

Facilities for Resource Sharing

(1) Narrowband Facilities

The narrowband facilities generally offer a transmission spectrum of less than 1 kilohertz. Transmission rates of up to 300 bits per second can be achieved. Switched facilities of this type include Western Union's TWX and Telex.

Fixed or leased narrowband facilities offered by the major communications common carriers are summarized in Table 5.1. The cost data is for illustrative purposes only and is subject to change. Rates shown are exclusive of any terminal equipment.

In general, the basic charges for a fixed or leased narrowband facility include these items:

1. Interexchange mileage charge -a monthly charge for the narrowband channel itself. (This charge is based on the distance between the common carrier's exchange offices.)
2. Service Terminal – a monthly charge applied for each city in which one or more terminal is located. This charge provides for the circuit from the local carrier exchange office to each of the customer's locations.
3. Installation – a one-time charge used to compensate the labor of installation or setup. It is usually equivalent to one month's termination charge.

Narrowband facilities are available as either half-duplex or full duplex channels. A half-duplex channel only permits transmission in one direction at a time. Two-way communication is possible, but not simultaneously, due to the fact that some circuits or components of the narrowband facilities are used for both transmission directions, thereby creating a common transmission path.

A full-duplex channel is capable of supporting simultaneous two-way communications because each transmission path has its own circuits or components totally isolated from the other transmission path.

Table 5.1. Narrowband Series 1000: Interchange Mileage Charges

Channel	Transmission	Type	Rate per mile per month ($)[a]				
			First 100 (0-100)	Next 150 (101-250)	Next 250 (251-500)	Next 500 (501-1000)	Over 1000 (1001 up)
Type 1001	Half-duplex	DC[b]	1.00	0.70	0.40	0.30	0.20
	Full-duplex	DC	1.10	0.77	0.44	0.33	0.22
Type 1002	Half-duplex	DC/CXR	1.40	0.98	0.56	0.42	0.28
	Full-duplex	DC/CXR	1.54	1.078	0.616	0.462	0.308
Type 1003	Half-duplex	DC/CXR	Same as Type 1002				
	Full-duplex	DC/CXR					
Type 1005	Half-duplex	DC/CXR	Same as Type 1002 plus 10%				
	Full-duplex	DC/CXR					
Type 1006	Half-duplex	CXR	Same as Type 1002 plus 15%				
	Full-duplex	CXR					

[a] These rates are subject to tariff changes and are reprsentative of FCC Tariff 260; they are based on usage 24 hr/day. 7 days/week. If the narrowband facility is between common carrier exchanges in the same state, the state tariff rates apply for both the interexchange mileage and the service terminals.

[b] DC refers to a telegraph grade line. A carrier line (CXR) requires data sets.

If an additional service terminal is required from the same common carrier exchange office on the same interexchange channel, the monthly rate is reduced for each service terminal added [Table 5.2].

Table 5.2. Narrowband Communications : Service Terminal and Installation Rates

Channel	Installation ($)[a]	1st service terminal in an exchange ($/ml)		Additional service terminals ($/ml)	
		Half-Duplex	Full-Duplex	Half-Duplex	Full-Duplex
Type 1001	10.00	25.00	27.50	7.50	8.25
Type 1002	10.00	25.00	27.50	7.50	8.25
Type 1003	10.00	25.00	27.50	7.50	8.25
Type 1005	10.00	27.50	30.25	8.25	9.08
Type 1006	10.00	31.25	34.37	9.38	10.32

(2) Voiceband Facilities

Generally voiceband facilities provide a transmission spectrum of three kilohertz. Depending on the type of data set utilized, a transmission rate of more than 9600 bits per second is possible; however, 2400 to 4800 bits per second is more common. The switched facilities of this type are the public voice switched network.

This bandwidth represents a compromise between intelligibility and cost. While the human voice has a considerably greater spectrum than 3000 Hertz, the ability of a human receiver (i.e., the human ear) to receive and understand the information content (intelligibility) is not appreciably enhanced by an increase in bandwidth.

(3) Fixed Voiceband Facilities

A fixed or leased voiceband facility is a communications channel permanently connected between two or more customer locations. This channel is normally provided on a full-time availability basis and is subject to a monthly charge based on direct airline distance between the points connected. (See Table 5.4.) In general, the basic charges for a fixed or leased voiceband facility include.

1. Interexchange mileage charge – a monthly charge for the voiceband channel itself, based on the distance between the common carrier's exchange offices.
2. Service terminal – a monthly charge that applies for each exchange in which one or more terminations are located. This charge covers the circuit from the common carrier's local exchange office to each customer location. It applies only to interstate services.
3. Installation – a one-time charge to compensate the labor of installation of setup.

Voiceband facilities are available as either half-duplex or full-duplex channels.

Table 5.3. Voiceband Series 3000 : Interstate Conditioning Rates

Conditioning level	Monthly charge ($)[a]
Type C1	
2-Point, no switching (per exchange)	5.00
2-Point, switching (per exchange)10.00	
Multipoint (per exchange 10.00	
Type C2	
2-Point, no switching (per exchange)	19.00
2-Point, switching (per exchange)28.00	
Multipoint (per exchange 28.00	
Type C3 (e.g. CCSA[b] systems)	
Local access line (each) 3.50	
Interexchange access line (per exchange)	13.75
Trunk line (per exchange) 12.00	
Type C4	
2-Point channel (1st station in exchange)	30.00
2-Point channel(each additional station in exchange	9.75
3-Point channel (1st station in exchange)	36.00
3-Point channel (each additional station in same exchange	9.75
Type C5	
2-Point channel (no switching per exchange)	37.00

Voiceband facilities are applicable to almost all library network needs except where large data rates require wideband facilities.

Because many long-distance interlibrary services can be provided over voiceband lines, it should be possible to rely upon the commercially available dial-up network for low-volume applications. The advantage of this approach is that it allows any library or user to connect directly with any other library using the commercial network's switching capability. However, when heavy traffic develops, cost savings can be achieved by using dedicated private faciiities with computers at the nodes performing the switching functions. Figure 6 illustrates the cost ratio between public and leased lines.

[4] Wideband Facilities

Wideband (or broadband) facilities have an extremely wide transmission spectrum that is capable of being used as a continuous spectrum or of being subdivided into channels equivalent to voiceband or narrowband facilities. The switched facilities Include Western Union Broadband Exchange Service and AT&T Data-Phone 50.

Table 5.4. Voiceband Series 4000 : Interexchange Mileage Rates

Miles	Rates per airline mile per month ($)	
	Half-Duplex	Full-Duplex
First 25 (1-25)	4.00	4.40
Next 75 (26-100)	2.80	3.08
Next 150 (101-250)	2.00	2.20
Next 250 (251-500)	1.40	1.54
Each additional mile (501 and over)	1.00	1.10

In the Auerbach Data Communications Reports, all communications facilities that have a frequency spectrum of 48 kilohertz and greater are classified as wideband. Wideband facilities are utilized for ultra-high data transmission or are channeled into a number of channels of lesser bandwidth, (i.e., derived channels). The practice of channeling is primarily to achieve a lower cost per derived channel mileage figure. The continuous spectrum wideband facilities are occasionally identified in terms of a transmission rate throughput in bits per second. This is not a totally incorrect method of definition, but it does assume that the terminating data sets are an integral part of the facility.

Fixed Wideband Facilities

A fixed or leased wideband facility is a communication channel permanently connected between two or more customer locations. These channels are normally provided with full-time availability and are subject to a monthly charge, although some types of video channels (Series 7000) may be installed on an hourly availability basis. The monthly charge is based on the airline mileage between the points connected. In general, basic charges for a fixed or leased voice band facilities include the followings:

1. **Interexchange mileage charge:** monthly charge for the wideband channel itself. This charge is based on the distance between the common carrier's exchange offices that are associated with the originating and terminating customer locations.
2. **Service terminal:** a monthly charge applied for each exchange termination. This charge provides for the circuit from the local common carrier's exchange office to each of the customer's locations. Wideband service terminals are categorized – and priced – by the type of channel, wideband or derived, at the customer's locations.

Table 5.5. Wideband Series 5000: Interexchange Mileage Rates

Type	Cost per airline mile per month ($)
5700	30.00
5800	85.00

Very large wideband facilities are necessary for certain applications. For example, the conventional television system uses a bandwidth of four megahertz, enough to accommodate 1000 simultaneous telephone conversations or 20,000 teleprinter channels. The cost is of course, quite high. However, in a library application, such as using a cathode ray tube (CRT) terminal to search a database, slow scan television requiring a bandwidth of only two kilohertz should be quite adequate.

Table 5.6. Wideband Series 5000: Service Terminals and Installation Rates (Wideband channels)

Terminal	1st station Installation ($)	1st station Monthly rate ($)	Each Additional station Monthly rate ($)
TYPE 5701			
10-20,000 Hz	200.00	425.00	300.00
40,800 bps	200.00	425.00	300.00
50,000 bps	200.00	425.00	300.00
TYPE 5703			
29-44 KHz	200.00	425.00	375.00
19.200 bps	200.00	425.00	375.00
TYPE 5706			
10-20,000 Hz	200.00	425.00	300.00
50,000 bps	200.00	425.00	-
TYPE 5751			
200-100,000 Hz	200.00	650.00	-
230,000 bps	200.00	650.00	-

Facsimile

Facsimile communications are secondary today to digital communications although a number of library networks have employed this technique [36, 37]. Facsimile allows for the transmission from one point to another of a full page image, including printed text, drawings, and photographs. Although considered by some as the sleeping giant of telecommunications, facsimile has several drawbacks in a library network environment. One is expense. Jackson reported facsimile transmission costs of from $7 to $31 per page at Penn State. Another drawback is the relatively slow speed of transmission over voice lines (about six minutes per page). Finally, a major facsimile roadblock is that most currently available facsimile devices lack the ability to scan directly from pages of a bound volume.

However, because of the ability of facsimile to transmit full text, microforms and both color and black and white photographs, it represents a potentially useful information transfer tool if its major drawbacks can be overcome.

Magnetic Tapes use for Bibliographic Data

While it may yet be some time before library networks exchange full text data in digital form, the dissemination of digitally encoded document surrogates among libraries and information centers is now becoming common. This technique represents a relatively low cost means by which libraries can share cataloging and other bibliographic data. With libraries having greater access to computing equipment, these low cost bibliographic records are gaining in popularity.

The potential products and services to be derived from the use of these readily available machine records are manifold, such as master data base building, computer search services, automatic preparation of catalog cards, and elimination of redundancy, cost, and effort in processing bibliographic records. Indeed, certain academic network operations such as those at the University of Pittsburgh, University of Georgia, Illinois Institute of Technology, and others have built their services around these machine-readable databases. One of the oldest cooperatives of this sort is the State University of New York (SUNY) regional biomedical communication network, which went into service in 1968. This network provides typewriter terminal search access to over one million medical journal citations from the National Library of Medicine's MEDLARS tapes to 16 medical centers.

These collections of bibliographic data in machine readable form represent a tremendously valuable resource of already prepared indexing and cataloging information in a variety of subject areas. A resource such as this cannot be overlooked in view of the tremendous costs and staffing problems encountered in the large scale indexing, abstracting, and cataloging of the literature and should serve as an incentive to networking so that libraries may band together to exploit these resources.

Standardization

A growing number of observers have expressed concern over the need to address compatibility problems both within, and even more importantly, between bibliographic and computer networks.

If effective and economical resource sharing is to be accomplished, there must be a means to ensure compatibility of information between the various network nodes. The only logical means to accomplish this is via standard, as Stevens points out.

It is to be noted; first, that system implementation will involve a great variety of decisions and choices to which standardization, compatibility, or convertibility require-ments will apply. Such choices include, but are not limited to, questions of hardware, software, data elements, data-content-representation conventions, formats, communication link requirements, routing requirements, file structuring, search structuring, machine and programming languages, documentation requirements, system accounting and performance measurement, error detection and error correction, and information control more generally, protection requirements, and the like.

Table 5.7. Roster of Organizations Regularly Distributing Bibliographic Records in Machine Readable Form (Magnetic Tape)

Organization	Records
American Geological Institute/ Geological Society of America	Bibliography and Index of Geology
American Institute of Aeronautics and Astronautics	International Aerospace Abstracts
American Petroleum Institute	Abstracts of Refining Literature Abstracts of Refining Patents
American Psychological Association	Psychological Abstracts
American Society of Mechanical Engineers	Applied Mechanics Reviews
American Society for Metals	Metals Abstracts
Armed Forces Pest Control Board	Military Entomology Information Service Bibliographic Information
Atomic Energy Commission	Nuclear Science Abstracts
Automation Instrument Data Service	Product Specifications for Electronic Instrumentation and Automation
Bio Science Information Service	BA Previews

Organization	Records
R.R. Bowker Company	Publisher's Weekly Forthcoming Books Paperbound Books in Print Subject Guide to Books in Print Children's Books for Schools and Libraries
CCM Information Sciences, Inc.	Pandex Weekly Tape Service
Chemical Abstracts Service	Chemical Abstracts Condensates Basic Journal Abstracts Chemical – Biological Activities Chemical Titles Polymer Science and Technology – P(atents) or J(ournals) Patent Concordance.
Clearinghouse for Federal Scientific and Technical Information	U.S. Government Besearch and Development Reports and Index
Defense Documentation Center	Technical Abstract Bulletin
Derwent Publications, Ltd.	Farmdoc Plasdoc Ringdoc
Educational Resources Information Center (ERIC)	Research in Education
Engineering Index, Inc.	Current Information Tapes for Engineers (CITE) Electrical/Electronics Plastics COMPENDEX
Paul De Haen, Inc.	De Haen Drug InformationServices
IFI/Plenum Data Corporation	Uniterm Index to U.S. Chemical Patents
Institute for Scientific Information	ISI Source Data Tapes ISI Citation Tapes Index Chemicus Registry System Automatic Subject Citations Alert (ASCA)
Institute of Textile Technology	Keyterm Index to Abstracts in the Textile Technology Digest
Library of Congress	MARC Tapes

(Contd.)

Organization	Records
M.I.T. Libraries (Project TIP)	The Current Journal Literature of Physics
National Aeronautics and Space Administration	Scientific and Technical Aerospace Reports
National Agricultural Library	Bibliography of Agriculture Subject and Corporate Author Indexes Pesticides Documentation Bulletin Citations International Tree Disease Register Herbicides Data File
National Library of Medicine	Index Medicus NLM Current Catalog
Preston Technical Abstracts Co.	Computer Tape for Searching the Gas Chromatographic Literature Nuclear Magnetic Resonance Literature Retrieval System
Project URBANDOC, Library, City University of New York	Bibliographic Records Related to Urban Planning and Renewal
Share Research Corporation	Abstracts of U.S. Government Report Literature (NASA, AEC, DOD, etc.) Citation to Journal Literature
State University of New York at Buffalo, Technical Information Dissemination Bureau	Bibliographic Information on U.S. Government Reports
U.S. Geological Survey	Abstracts of North American Geology
University of Michigan	VELA Seismic Information Analysis Center Citations
University of Tulsa	Petroleum Abstracts (Exploration/ development/Production Literature and Patents)

The recognition of the importance of standards by the United States Government can be seen in the publication of the *Federal Information.*

Conclusion

Technology can foster the creation of resource sharing networks, which can achieve economy by eliminating redundancy while offering network users an expanded scope of services through their local library node.

However, not all libraries, nor library networks, have yet availed themselves of the fruits of modern technology, some of which have been summarized in the preceding pages. This appears to be particularly true in Pennysylvania where there has been surprisingly little automated network development for such a large state.

The gap between conventional, and often outmoded, libraries and modern information systems must be bridged quickly, for the challenge to libraries to keep pace with the growing volume of information has already been clearly stated. Academic library collections expanded by 50% from 1966 to 1970 [45]. Many libraries have not met this challenge and many more will also fail unless we can give each library, no matter how limited its scope, the opportunity to exploit the information processing potential of the computer and its concomitant technology.

Yet a paradox exists with respect to library automation activities. Which librarians of every nature are exhibiting an intense and increasing interest in the application of information technology library operations, relatively few are actually participating in "hands on" mechanization activity. It appears that the imposing economic, administrative, educational, and staffing problems encountered in mechanizing library operations have led many librarians to adopt a "wait and see" attitude with respect to automation. This dilemma is not in the best interests of the American library community.

Rather than wait, librarians should immediately begin to study and evaluate the state of the art of information technology to determine how their needs can be met and their services improved. They should be aware of the new developments in the area of memory technology that are forcing information storage costs down. They should investigate the capabilities of available software which the may be able to plug into their own systems without extensive modifications, particularly software which has proven itself in a library network environment such as OCLC's. The capabilities of computers and their peripheral devices should be evaluated on a cost benefit basis. The now emerging specialized common carriers, such as Datran and MCI, should be monitored to determine if their rates will make remote telecommunications more attractive.

This evaluation should be conducted in the context of a realistic statement of the library's service needs and economic and administrative constraints. Only in this way will a library of a group of libraries be able to accurately determine when and how information technology can be employed.

Many librarians have indeed conducted such analyses on their own and have found that while the technology is now available to satisfy their needs, they do not have the resources to fully exploit it. Byrn [46] brings this out when he cites as the three most prevailing reasons for the relative lack of progress in university library automation:

1. Critical lack of properly skilled personnel
2. A shortage of funds available
3. Lack of facilities to properly carry out a meaningful automation program (including problems in dealing with outside support)

The sharing of information, information processing, information storage, and information transmission facilities among a number of libraries via a network is technically feasible, in addition it will distribute cost and, in turn, diminish the burden on the individual library center. Cooperative information processing activities also put the participants in a better position to impose their demands on the huge and occasionally unsympathetic hardware, software, and communication suppliers.

The technology to facilitate cooperative resource sharing is now available. There are many economic, administrative and service incentives for a cooperative approach to exploiting this technology. However, because technology utilization doesn't come cheapy, in terms of both investment of dollar and intellectual resources, the successful utilization of technology on a cooperative basis requires much detailed planning and analysis, plus a firm commitment from the participants.

The technology to allow implementation to automated library networks is here and is available at prices that are becoming more and more attractive. However, to exploit this technology effectively the librarian should be aware of the relevant state of the art in information storage, information processing and information transfer. As existing networks have demonstrated, this investment can yield significant returns.

However, it appears that librarians may have to rely on their own resources for this investment as government supplied R & D funds are becoming quite scarce. Libraries will have to band together voluntarily to share resources, staff, and know-how. An effective means of accomplishing this can be the establishment of relatively small regional cooperatives, which could serve as pilot test beds for both the applications of information technology and the administrative efficacy of multilibrary resource sharing. Those pilot cooperatives that prove feasible can serve as models which can be expanded and replicated elsewhere with appropriate regional modifications. This activity will, of necessity, require a concerted cooperative effort on the part of librarians, information systems architects, and the administration of the involved libraries' patent organization if it is to succeed. Each of these groups must contribute not only its know-how, but its support, both moral and financial, and must effectively employ the collective experience of others who have addressed these problems in the past.

6

COMPUTERIZE INFORMATION SYSTEM

Introduction

This tremendous growth of information had resulted in a host of problems in the storage and transfer of information-the most affected being the users and the intermediaries. Developments in Information Technology offered solutions to many of the problems in harnessing information. Creation of Online Information Systems and Services is a landmark in this path, which facilitates faster and effective access to information. It opened up a new era in the information transfer process from a very slow and conventional methods of accessing a limited range of information to an instantaneous, electronic access to a near exhaustive world literature.

Components of the System

The major component of an online Information system are INFORMATION, COMPUTERS and COMMUNICATIONS. In an Online system facility, the information stored in computer readable form, known as Database, is accessed by the remotely stationed users through telecommunication lines using a telex or computer terminal.

The kinds of information searchable can be bibliographic, numeric or full text. Majority of the databases accessible online at present, however, belong to bibliographic databases. There are currently about four thousand online searchable databases the world over. These databases are produced by Governmental Agencies, Publishers, Professional Societies, Libraries and Information Centers, etc. A few major databases with the names of their producers are listed below:

CA SEARCH	American Chemical Society, Ohio
MEDLINE	U.S. National Library of Medicine
BIOSIS	BIOSIS, Philadelphia
METADEX	ASM International, Ohio/TMS, London
COMPENDEX	Engineering Information Inc., New York
INSPEC	IEE, London

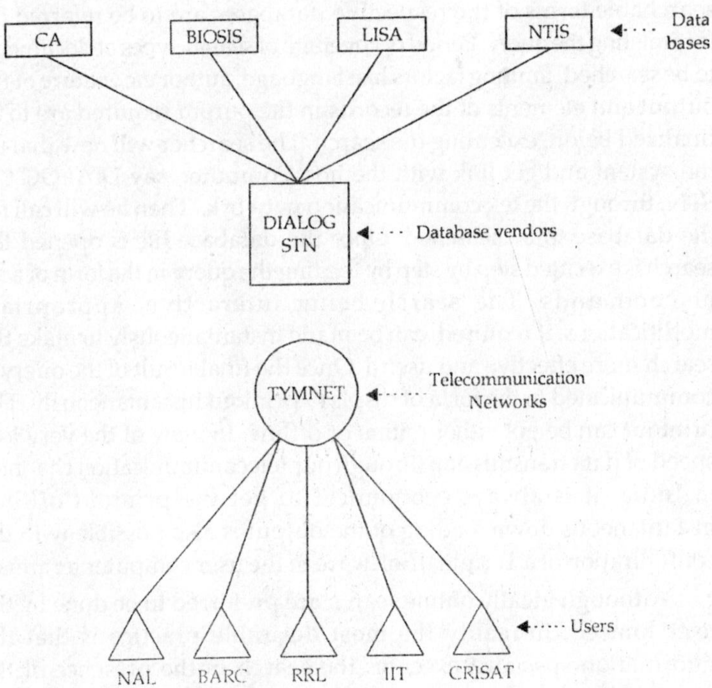

Database vendors constitute an important link in the online information system; Databases leased by these vendors are stored in their host computers, which are accessed by the users from remote stations. DIALOG, STN, PERGAMON INFOLINE are some such vendors. Of these, DIALOG has the largest number of Databases. Started with a single database in 1969, DIALOG now provides more than 400 databases. As in other parts of the world, majority of the online community in India also are the customers of DIALOG.

Searching

Steps involved in doing an Online Bibliographic Information Search may be examined now. The user should have the PASSWORD of the concerned database vendor for using the online system. The most suited database (s) for the topic of search has to be identified first. The topic to be searched has to be analyzed and a search query has to be formulated. This will be an expression in the form of a set of KEYWORDS/ DESCRIPTORS with appropriate combination as warranted by using the Boolean search logic. Search guides and searchable terms of the respective databases are to be referred for formulating the query. Period of coverage of search, types of documents to be searched, limiting factors like language, author etc., nature of the output and elements of the records in the output required are to be finalized before executing the search. The searcher will now dial up the system and get link with the host computer, say DIALOG OR STN, through the telecommunication network. Then he will call for the database to be searched. Once the database file is opened the search is executed step by step by feeding the query in the form of a set of commands. The search being interactive, appropriate modifications, if required, can be made instantaneously to make the search more effective and useful. Once the final result of the query is communicated to the form of display/printout instantaneously. The printout can be got either online or offline. In view of the very low speed of data transmission through our telecommunication channels in India, it is always economical to get the printout offline, instantaneous down loading of the output is also possible with the configuration of a Terminal Software in the user computer terminal.

Although ideally online search are preferred to be done by the user himself, in reality the most desirable practice is that the information specialist executes the search in the presence of the user.

Services for Searching

Online information services include supply of specific information, current and retrospective bibliographic information. SDI service, Online document ordering and supply service etc.

1. Cost

The cost of online search includes two segments. The first one is the Systems cost and the second, the Telecommunication cost. Systems cost include connect time charges and the output/printout cost. Both the costs vary from database to database. Print out cost further varies on the basis of Format options.

The Indian Scene

The situation in India on the use of online systems and creation of databases is not very encouraging. The landmark in the development in the country was the feasibility demonstration conducted in the 1970s in Bombay from where ESRIN (Rome) was accessed. The second major event was the Telesearch-I project of NAL, Bangalore under which for about two years (1986-87) the online search service was operational with the facility to access International S & T databases and databanks held by ESA/IRS at Esrin, via land and satellite dedicated links. This had to be abandoned owing to the heavy investments-both initial and recurring costs and a relatively poor response from the user community. The second phase of the system is now operational at NAL, Bangalore under which DIALOG is accessed online under the NACID program of NISSAT. This program called Telesearch-II will continue till March 1990. In addition to the five NACID centers functional at present under the NISSAT program a number of other establishments, most in the S & T sector, are regularly doing online information search of international databases. ICRISAT, Hyderabad and BHEL, Hyderabad were two centers where online system was operational in the early period. RRL. Trivandrum is another institution where the system is operational without the assistance of any external agency like NISSAT. The commenced the online search service in 1985. Initially, delegated searches were made. Since 1987 they have been doing direct online search through DIALOG, California. M/s. Information (India) Private Limited, Bangalore has also made commendable contributions in the development of online systems facility in our country by way of either operational services and educational programs.

Currently, leased tapes are available in India on INSPEC, BIOSIS, MATHOCI, GEOREFF, CASEARCH, COMPENDEX, MEDLARS, METADEX, INIS, AGRIS, IMPADOC, INFORTERRA, etc. But the services are limited to only certain institutions and areas. The number of users are also very much limited. Efforts in the Indian scene are thus found to be fragmented which result in high costs, poor quality, duplication and waste of resources. The situation is somewhat similar to the condition prevailing in Europe in the 1960s. A team of European Community experts appointed to study the situation in India in their report published in 1988 had remarked "Important infrastructure elements such as Networks, Hosts, Indian databases, Marketing of foreign information are still not in place. Absence of a coherent infrastructure and policy framework" is the basic problems. Setting up of a multifunctional host as the National Focal Point was recommended by the experts.

It is heartening to note that some positive measures are now being adopted to promote and develop online systems and service facilities in India. Project Aristotle, initiated by Videsh Sanchar Nigam Ltd., Bombay in association with a host of other national agencies is an important step. The program envisages creation, marketing and networking of Indian databases, easy access to international databases etc. Gateway packet switching service GPSS launched in the last quarter of 1988 by VSN Limited, Bombay provides an inexpensive and reliable link to TYMNET AND TELENET. If we are using a 1200 bps line, it might cost us in the range of Rs. 10-20 per minute compared to the earlier rate of Rs. 75/- per minute towards telecommunication charges.

The Indian condition is quite fertile for the growth of online information system. A quantitative study of the Indian Subscriptions to hard copy versions numbering to hundreds will certainly reveal that the total subscription cost will car exceed the cost of leasing one copy of the online version. In a systematic collection development for the country, online will prove to be more economic and efficient than the traditional mode of information retrieval.

Trends in Future

CD-ROM, the latest in the information technology is really going to be a threat to the present online systems. Unlike the microfilm/microfische revolution in the document collection in libraries, CD-ROM is going to create a tremendous impact in the information storage and retrieval with the transformation of information search from ONLINE to ONDISC. However, a combination of CD-ROM and online system facility could be a more appropriate choice for India.

7

Resource Sharing Through Computer Networks in Higher Education

If actually sharing library resources were as simple as saying "do it now" there would be no need for further discussion. I could terminate this chapter at this point, you could stop reading, and resource sharing could begin tomorrow. Unfortunately, the problem is not that simple and conferences are badly needed to reach a consensus on when and how libraries can most effectively accomplish the sharing of resources.

As already discussed, a basic problem facing libraries today is the tremendous increase in available information - not only the absolute quantity of that information, but the rate at which new information is being produced. In addition, library patrons are becoming increasingly interested in being provided with better tools for accessing this information.

Traditional library methods have barely been able to cope with these increased requirements, and library budgets have had difficulty keeping up with the ever-increasing spiral of library costs. The Purdue study referenced earlier points out that for the past several decades, the average academic research library collection has been doubling in size every 16 to 17 years and its total expenditures have been doubling about every 7 years. And yet, despite increasing expenditures and acquisitions, the number of volumes per student in American college and university libraries actually declined from 52.4 to 43.5 volumes over the 12 – year period from 1960 to 1972. Clearly the continuing effectiveness and even the survival of libraries will depend in large measure upon their ability simultaneously to combat rising costs and to provide the increased services which are desired. This will make resource sharing essential.

What is Resource Sharing?

What do I mean by resource sharing? First, the sharing of library materials and of the professional talent which organize and maintains those materials. Second, sharing in the setting of priorities and the determination of policies under which this will be done. Third, sharing in the planning, conduct and support of research and development for ways of handling resource-sharing better. Further, I mean resource sharing in completely new ways now made possible by advances in computer and communications technology.

The amazing capabilities of the computer are well known and have been used in a variety of library applications. But significant cost saving from resource sharing requires also the communication between libraries that computer networks provide. This newly available networking technology has the potential of offering the breakthrough in the library and information science field that is needed to lower unit costs and strengthen services, because it offers a way in which technology can be combined with the cooperative efforts of a group of libraries.

Some savings have been affected in the past through libraries agreeing to work together and make reciprocal use of their resources. Savings have also resulted from the introduction of technology into individual libraries. However, it is only when cooperation is combined with technology as in the case of computer networks, that the total savings will be really significant.

Since the technology and are of networking are recent developments, I should like to devote most of my discussion to this facet of resource sharing.

By happy coincidence, Education just conducted for the National Science Foundation three seminars on computer networking which brought together over 150 people with a variety of backgrounds and expertise. Their competence and wisdom far exceed my own and I am therefore going to make extensive use of the draft of their report.

"Articulation of the possibilities of computer networks is not what is new. That goes back to the early 1960's and before. Nor is the implementation and operation of networks new. Many working networks have been in evidence for several years now, both commercially and in universities. What is new is the unmistakable recognition, bordering on a sense of the inevitable, that networks are now practical and are here to stay... It is time to sit up, take notice, and do some hard-nosed comparative analysis".

The current mode of autonomous, self-sufficient operation in the provision of computing and information services is frequently wasteful, deficient, and unresponsive to users' needs.

"The waste was said to come about because of duplication, redundancy of effort from one installation to another, incompatibilities, other impediments to the sharing of resources, and underutilization of installed equipment. Yet, simultaneously, there was thought to be much unsatisfied pent-up demand for computer and information services, as well as widespread unhappiness with the general level of documentation, program support, and user assistance. Complaints were voiced about the relative lack of uniform standards and the paucity of information on what programs and data are available and how to get and use them.

Networking does not in and of itself offer a solution to current deficiencies. What it does offer is a promising vehicle with which to bring about important changes in user practices, institutional procedures, and government policy that can lead to effective solutions.

"Thus, more critical than whether networking is developed and applied is how it is developed and applied. For example networking emphasizes the need for standards and good documentation. Unless effective mechanisms are developed and strong measures taken in networking to ensure that suitable standards and documentation are developed, present inadequacies could get worse, not better."

Participants considered this to be the right time for top level decision makers at different institutions to meet and begin thinking about how large-scale networks might look and work. Officials must question seriously and honesty how well computing and information services are currently supplied, how well users are served, the historical reasons for the present mode of operation, how networks and other fast-advancing technologies might improve the operation, and what changes in government policy and institutional attitudes would be required or helpful in bringing about this improvement. With this in mind, it is recommended that.

Conclusion

The conclusion of the Seminar participants that the technology for computer networking is available here and now should perhaps have some supporting evidence. It is being used in more than 20 regional networks whose development has been supported by the National Science Foundation. There are operating networks centered at Dartmouth College, the University of Iowa, Illinois Institute of Technology, the University of Texas and the Washington State University. The Triangle Universities Computation Center in North Carolina provides computer services to the North Carolina State University, University of North Carolina and duke University. The North Carolina Educational Computing Service also provides a mechanism through which computer programs developed at one school can be shared with the others. "The MERIT Network is an arrangement through which the University of Michigan, Michigan State, and Wayne State University can share resources. UNI-COLL is an effort by the University City Science Center of Philadelphia to operate a combined computation center for some twenty-seven colleges and universities in the Delaware Valley." The University of Pennsylvania has turned over its large IBM computer to UNI-COLL and the other colleges in the consortium have access to it through a network.

Several states either already have or are developing statewide computer networks (California, Illinois, New Jersey, New York, Minnesota, Oregon, and Florida). A current EDUCOM study, sponsored by the Exxon Education Foundation, will examine the extent to which state agencies have been assuming responsibility for coordinating the acquisition of computing resources for state college and universities. It will also facilitate and encourage the sharing of information among the states and permit and evaluation to be made of the impact of these developments on computing in higher education and on the relationship between educational and governmental agencies.

The Advanced Research Projects Agency of the Department of Defense has developed the ARPANET, a national network of computers of leading universities and research organizations, which permits heterogeneous computers to communicate with one another in a technologically effective and economical manner using a technology referred to by its developers as "packet switching." The use of high speed (50 kilobit per second) communications lines, and the efficient utilization of those lines, makes the transfer of textual materials both practical and economical. The end-to-end delay in transferring a full screen of information over the ARPANET is less than half a second and this has exciting possibilities for library use.

Originally the exclusive province of researchers in computer science, the ARPANET is being used more and more as a vehicle for sharing computer resources. The IBM 360/91 computer at UCLA receives 25% of its total revenue from network customers within the first year of accepting and the Burroughs 6700 at the University of California at San Diego receives 20%. The University of Illinois gave up its Burroughs 6700 computer and now uses the one at the University of California at San Diego. The cost for getting through the network the same amount of computing formerly provided by the Burroughs computer is reported to be one-third of the amount it cost Illinois to have its own machine.

Harvard has returned its large IBM computer to the manufacturer and greatly reduced its central computing facility. Harvard originally planned to develop a joint computer center with MIT, but this was replaced by an arrangement through which Harvard essentially became a customer of MIT. Most recently Harvard has set out to shop nationally for the best service available for each application which can then be secured through ARPANET or other network facilities directly from the computer center which developed the service.

The National Library of Medicine has established a service called MEDLINE. It uses TYMNET facilities and permits medical researchers throughout the country to have on-line access to over 400,000 citations to articles from about 1200 major journal indexed for Index Medicus. This is almost 60% of the citations printed since January 1, 1970.

The Ohio College Library Center is demonstrating the specific advantages of networking for academic libraries. The heart of this system is a computer based, on-line shared catalog which uses MARC II tapes supplied by the library of Congress and cataloging data input by member libraries. This system produces library catalog cards at a cost considerably below that required by most existing manual methods and has been on-line since October 1911. By allowing each member library to specify its own card format, the system is one of few applications which use the computer as an instrument for facilitating a healthy diversity rather than as a club to enforce rigid conformity.

There are some seven regions which are actively considering replication of the OCLC System. However, the problem of how a system which was set up in a single state can become a national federation of regional systems each of which will have a voice in determining policy has not yet been addressed, let alone solved - and this leads into the critical question.

If networking technology is not only available but is being used and the advantages of resource sharing through computer networks are even being demonstrated in particular library applications, why then is this technology not being applied more generally to solving the problems of the library?

The published report of the study of libraries and information technology which was sponsored by the National Academy of Sciences speaks to this question:

"The primary bar to development of national computer-based library and information systems is no longer basically a technology feasibility problem. Rather, it is the combination of complex institutional and organizational human-related problems and the inadequate economic/value system associated with these activities".

In thinking about this problem I have found it useful to classify these inhibiting factors under three broad headings - organizational, psychological and economic.

The National Academy of Sciences report also observed that "... science policy must assume a much more effective role in stimulating public and private actions to weld the present localized and fragmentary efforts into nationally coherent programs". In short, what is needed is organization.

The feeling on the part of the participants in the Networking Seminars that "now is the time for institutions of research and education of commit themselves to reexamine, compare, analyze, plan, and begin to organize and coordinate their actions with respect to computing and information services" led to the most action directed and most encompassing recommendation of their report.

"The Council should be a working group rather than an associational organization of representatives. Its membership should include people from institutions of higher education, research centers, information service groups, libraries, and laboratories (including those of profit-making corporations), selected on the basis of their experience, expertise, and ability to contribute not only to the deliberations and mission of the Council, but also to the national networking arrangements to which the activities of the Council might lead... The Council might be set up for a five-year term to

Commission studies, tests, and experiments exploring the problems and prospects for national networkings;

Draft a plan for the formation of subnets and appoint panels to identify resources;

Stimulate planning and organizational activities that will provide orderly transition to a large-scale facilitating network operation if one is deemed desirable;

Recruit entrepreneurial activists knowledgeable about networking to go out, answer questions, determine interest, and earliest support for the work of the Council;

Inform institutions about plans and future possibilities to help them prepare, adjust, and avoid disruption and surprise;

Recommend an organizational structure for national networking in the period beyond the life of the Council.

"The members of the Council might be organizations and institutions, each served by two officials: Normally one would be the president, chancellor, provost, senior vice president, or director at the topmost level of organizational authority at a point where the financial, operating, and planning responsibilities of the organization meet. The second would be someone in a position that brings him in contact with a broad cross-section of the users of information and computing services; for example, the director of research, the coordinator of computing resources, or the director of computing activities. With the proviso that the Council be a working group, its organizational membership should be as broadly based as possible. It should be supported by a substantial financial contribution from each member that expresses the member's commitment and gives the Council the financial base it must have to commence its activities.

Another factor inhibiting the use of technology in the library area is the psychological one. We are all more or less creatures of habit and much prefer to stick with the known rather than venture too far into uncharted waters. We are also somewhat reluctant to exchange procedures which have worked and are still working for new procedures of uncertain merit and even more uncertain expense.

But there are some indications that the fundamental psychological inhibitions to resource sharing are being overcome. As the librarian at a leading academic research library has written to me.

"At long last, I think it safe to say that there is general recognition, at least on the part of librarians, that any attempt at local self-sufficiency in library collections is simply unrealistic. Increasingly over recent decades, no libraries, not even the very largest, have been able to provide in themselves all the resources required by their scholarly clienteles.

Finally, there are some formidable economic inhibitions, which must be overcome if there is to be sharing of library resources through a computer network. Developing such a network takes a period of years and during the transitional period, the existing system must still be maintained. This requires a double expenditure of funds, maintaining the old while at the same time inaugurating the new. In addition, for many state systems, there are prohibitions against spending money outside the borders of the state, which will somehow have to be overcome if a truly national network is to emerge.

The financial stringencies under which most colleges and universities are operating today make the decision to cooperate and share resources a very difficult one, even though in the long run this will result in economies. It takes a farsighted stance and real courage in these times of financial shortages to divert money from satisfying pressing current needs to research on sharing resources – since the short-term consequences frequently loom larger than the long-range benefits.

To sum up, now is the time to extend resource sharing among libraries. What is needed is a commitment on the part of librarians and top university administrators who recognize the opportunities for resource sharing inherent in computer networking and have the courage to invest in long-range efforts that will benefit not only individual libraries, but ultimately all of higher education.

The technology which will permit greatly increased sharing of library resources by means of computer networks is here, but is only beginning to be applied to the solution of the problems facing academic libraries.

Traditional library methods will have to be modified to include the new technology of computer networking. Even the largest libraries will no longer be able to amass collections, which are completely self-sufficient. The rising volume of information and rising level of costs are so great that only through cooperation and the sharing of resources will libraries be able to cope.

8

Data Communication Through Packet Switching

Data Communication in telecommunications in India started in the seventies with the provision of leased data circuits.

With the growth of computers, largely facilitated by cheap indigenous microprocessor based systems, computer and allied computer communications activity has taken a leap. Department of telecommunications has come forward with data on Public Switched Telephone Network (PSTN) since the early eighties. Simultaneously, it has embarked on a plan of action to introduce switched data network spread all over the country. The technology of switching, proposed to be adopted (Packet Switching), is different from that used in telephone switching. Besides, the data switching technology requires development of interfaces on user computers, which are compatible.

To meet both the requirements and to get 'hands-on' experience in this new field, Department of Telecommuni-cations has set up an experimental network with the help of Telecommunications Consultant India Limited (TCIL) covering New Delhi, Bombay and Madras cities, using indigenously available computers (IDM S-3250) to work as exchange at these locations. Trials are also being conducted on an experimental circuit switched data network at 300 bps with a limited number of subscribers between Delhi and Bombay. This network is formed from existing electronic telex exchanges (ETX) at these two places.

After successful initial trials with a few subscribers, the Telecommunication Research Center of the Department of Telecommunications introduced India's first Packet Switching Data Network (PSDN) on 11th June 1986 at New Delhi. This is a these node network set up on an experimental basis by close cooperation between the Telecommunication Research Centre (TRC) and TCIL utilizing indigenous computers and equipment.

In the initial trial stages, services will be offered to a limited number of subscribers at Delhi, Bombay and Madras on a free of charge basis which would enable the Department of Telecommunications to collect valuable data on the type, pattern and volume of traffic and also to enable the subscribers to assess the services and suggest improvement/changes for greater utility. The entire data communication software of this service has been developed by TCIL. It includes:

1. Switching Software,
2. Packet assembler/dissembler (PAD) software,
3. Electronic Mail Box software.

Broadly, the network will provide three types of facilities-message transfer, interactive computer access and computer-computer communication. Small microcomputers can access larger databases or can do the data processing on a remotely located computer. The transfer of files from the terminal/micro-computer to any other computer or vice versa is possible. Of special interest is the use of a telex machine as a computer terminal, which provides a comparatively cheap mode of data processing capability for low volume users.

Types of Packet Switching

1. *Access through Public Switched Telephone Network (PSTN) 300 bpsl 1200 bps:* These subscribers can be existing PSTN subscribers or newly enrolled subscribers. This service will be provided for 300 bps/1200 bps full duplex working. PSTN subscribers who are licensed for access to data network will be provided outgoing facility only by dialing 6 or 7 digits telephone numbers.
2. *1200 bps Asynchronous Full Duplex working connected through leased lines:* This facility will be provided to the subscribers with

high volume data traffic like those who want to connect a computer for data communications and data processing. Computers will be connected at terminals to the data network and remote data processing will be possible through the data network.

3. *Electronic Mail Box:* This is a store and retrieve facility. This package is integrated with PAD so that this facility could be used by PSTN, telex or leased lines.
4. *Additional services to be introduced-Telex access-2400 bps Full Duplex Synchronous working:* For providing this data service to the existing telex subscribers, there is no additional investment towards equipment at subscriber's premises. The teleprinter will be used as data terminal. There will be a specific number provided for this service and the telex subscribers should dial this number for accessing the data network.

Procedures for Packet Switching

Each subscriber using the network and accessing through a telephone call will be allotted a unique code called the network user identity (NUI) for reasons of security and charging, etc. This code is decided by himself. Directly connected subscribers do not require this as they are permanently wired to the exchange whereas the will have a network user address (NUA).

1. Subscribers in the network with PSTN access dial the local telephone number of the 'node' as in an ordinary telephone call. He is connected to the 'node' through the 'telephone call' using modems. Further calling and data exchange are done during the telephone call using NUIs and NUAs.
2. Subscribers directly connected to the network make calls on the network straightaway.
3. Electronic mail facility in the network is used by accessing the node and subsequently conversing with the electronic mail software.

Features of the Data Service

1. Data access PSTN subscribers whose telephone lines are with or without STD facility can get access to the Electronic Mail Box facility to local/distant stations. This facility is

particularly useful because incoming access is barred for PSTN subscribers.

2. Repeat dialing attempts on the already busy network will be completely eliminated because of the storage facilities provided in the system. The subscriber has to dial a local number only for accessing the data network. This will reduce congestion and improve the speed with which long distance communications can take place. The ineffective calls due to called number remaining busy during the peak hour will be taken care of by the network which will smoothen the peak load by storing the messages and passing on to the destination off-peak periods.
3. Exchange of messages between telephone subscribers (PSTN), telex subscribers and dedicated leased line users will be possible because of the inter-working facilities provided by the network.
4. The lines will have both inter-active working and file transfer capabilities. Small micro computers can access larger data bases or can do the data processing on a remotely located computer. The transfer of files from the terminal/micro computer to any other computer and vice versa is possible. Using a telex machine as a computer terminal provides a cheap mode of data processing capability, which can be used to the maximum extent by schools and colleges for imparting knowledge on computer programming to the students.

9

Networking for Restoring Library Ecology

Our new computerized systems have been successful as far as the go. In some cases the have added a new dimension to our communications capability, but we can no longer close our eyes to the fact that this increased capability at one point in the information cycle is not matched throughout the cycle. The resulting imbalance is upsetting the operating ecology of many information service operations. In simple terms, we have stimulated with our information services more demand for documents than our delivery systems can supply.

As one who is involved from an operating standpoint with the balanced ecology of a biomedical information network, I am very seriously concerned. On the other hand, I am still confident that the present anomalies in our capabilities will be adjusted by upgrading the total network capability, beginning with the use of our latest technological advances to strengthen the subsystems and systems making up the network. I plan to expand on this thesis shortly, but before I do, let me provide my simple answer to the question of when to share resources. The answer is now.

Complete self-sufficiency in the library world is no longer either possible or desirable. Sharply rising costs coupled with tight budgets are compelling forces none of us can ignore, and the concept of sharing is generally accepted today as fundamental to our continuing capacity to provide economically the type, quality, and volume of information service required by our customers. We all seem to agree on the "why" and I suspect on the "when." The major difficulty, of course, comes in the "how," and my concern about the present imbalance in the total information process cuts across both the "when" and the "how" of resource sharing.

Let me expand briefly on this concern of mine. In the last 20 years, information science has concentrated on information retrieval methods for pulling from a large information base the subset of specific documents that are revelent to a particular information need. Our so-called retrieval systems are being computerized. Information about documents, not the documents themselves, is stored and manipulated in the computer. Some of our systems depend on detailed indexing using controlled vocabularies. Others have computerized full text SCAN capabilities. In fact, our ability to make users aware of documents the may need has expanded greatly. The knowledge of what materials exist stimulates requests for more information among library users, and indeed has overloaded the capacity of many libraries to deliver the documents so effectively advertised by information retrieval systems.

Library Tools

All of the information about documents which indexing and current awareness tools present to our library users is of no consequence if the user cannot have access to the documents themselves. "No matter how elegant our network of our retrieval systems for medical (or any other kind of) information become, the nub of the matter remains getting the information to the users. In the library vernacular – 'document delivery". In the 7th Annual Review of Information Science and Technology we are told that document delivery and the problems of accomplishing it receive precious little attention in the open literature well makes the point that "...new information systems for alerting and for storage and retrieval have recently monopolized the limelight. Only a few information managers and projects such as MIT's Intrex have clearly pointed out that providing pertinent documents is also vital". We might restate this by saying that it is crucial that libraries provide requested documents promptly and economically, that is a library's job.

And yet, as surprising as it may seem, I know of a number of cases not in the medical area where access to and use of the computerized information retrieval systems is being sharply curtailed by the librarians simply because of the inability of the librarians to deliver the requested material on any kind of reasonable schedule. This is almost analogous to having heavily traveled eight-lane super highway feed into a two-lane road, resulting in huge traffic problems. To me, such a situation is deplorable. When one considers the human factors – namely, the overworked library staffs – it is understandable, but nevertheless, it is still deplorable. Fortunately this situation is not yet typical of all our libraries, but it is worsening, and as we now start interconnecting and networking the systems, the severity of the problem is rising exponentially. The growing demand for the librarian to borrow more and more source materials using our current outdated methods is creating burdensome workloads which have to be attended to at the expense of other pressing library duties. If the deterioration continues it will soon reach the critical stage.

Interlibrary loans, including the provision of photocopies in lieu of papers, is an old and established practice. Many libraries have joined in listing their holdings in Union lists of serials and Union catalogs on a local, national. Or even discipline basis. These Union lists and agreements to share the holdings the cover in effect constitute library networks. In libraries and Information Technology: A National System Challenge, the Information System Panel of the Computer Science and Engineering Board of the National Academy of Sciences stated that:

> *...the library function contains the "memory" of national information systems. The current embodiment of this memory is in the wide range of the large national libraries, major academic and research libraries, public libraries, school libraries and so on, and various information collections used in support of industry, government and education.*

Inter Library Loan

The National Commission and the National Science Foundation are both concerned with this resource sharing problem and have commissioned studies with the Association of Research Libraries which may lead to a network of comprehensive national, regional, or even disciplinary depository literature collections to be shared by participating libraries. Perhaps this type of network of major lending libraries will prove to be more effective than the status quo, even using today's not too efficient United States Mail Service for the transmission and delivery of documents.

There are a number of major resource sharing efforts under way. Let us look at one with which I am most familiar. At the National Library of Medicine we have established a national resource sharing network of medical libraries. This network, of course, deals with a limited area of knowledge, concentrating on biomedicine.

Perhaps a brief word about this network, which admittedly is in its early stages of development, well provide some insight into a "real-life" effort currently underway. It is a network with many of the strengths and weaknesses which have been highlighted in proceeding chapters but at the same time it is one organization's attempt to do something about resource sharing now.

The Library, which was established in 1836, now houses the largest and finest collection of health sciences literature in the world – 1,300,000 volumes and 20,000 serials. Into our computerized bibliographic control system we will add this year approximately a quarter of a million citations from the world's medical literature. Photocomposing equipment will produce from the resultant machine-readable data base Index Medicus, Current Catalog, and a number of recurring bibliographies.

Medical Library Loan

The backbone of the medical library network is MEDLINE, an on-line, real time bibliographic searching system, the MEDLINE data base contains 400,000 citations to articles from the most important 1200 to 2400 journals indexed in Index Medicus since January 1970. It is in effect a core data base and one which we have found to be most effective as well as economical to operate.

MEDLINE is queried by remote access terminals via a commercial communications network operated by the Tymshare Corporation with nodes in 40 cities. The MEDLINE terminal operator dials the nearest node city and is automatically connected to the NLM data-base and computer in Bethesda, Maryland. An on-line news file alerts all users to MEDLINE systems developments, changes in the databases, and scheduling information. The commercial communications network makes effective national coverage possible and economical, and at the same time provides the connection to the data bases of other organizations commercially available on the Tymshare network. For example, anyone with a MEDLINE terminal may also, for a fee, have access to the ERIC data base developed by the Office of Education. Data bases produced by the Chemical Abstract Service are also accessible on Tymshare. NLM itself provides six more data bases to MEDLINE users:

1. SDILINE functions as MEDLINE's current awareness service.
2. COMPFILE, available at selected hours, makes it possible to search citations from the remaining 1200 journals covered in Index Medicus but not in MEDLINE.
3. BACKFILE furnishes access to citations older than the MEDLINE data base
4. CATLINE carries monographic cataloging information produced by NLM and NLM'S cooperative cataloging partners.
5. SERLINE, a data base of approximately 6300 substantial serial titles in the field of biomedicine, presents cataloging information and locator codes to aid all participating medical libraries in finding the nearest source of procurement for a periodical available on interlibrary loan.

The MEDLINE network with its multiple data bases is the fundamental tools in the Regional Medical Library Program, which is a hierarchical network of libraries that supplies document delivery in the form of interlibrary loan of monographs and photocopy of journal articles. The Regional Medical Library program divides the country geographically into eleven regions, each serviced by a Regional Medical Library (RML). The basic units, or bottom layer of the pyramid, and the libraries in community hospitals, clinics, colleges with health science education programs, and other health related agencies such as research organizations or governmental agencies. The second layer is composed of the resource libraries, which are generally the well-stocked libraries of major medical schools. Each region is headed by its RML. The RML's are also responsible for coordinating MEDLINE service in the regions. MEDLINE service began with the RML's and resource libraries and is being extended to larger hospitals and other institutions.

Requests for documents move upward through the network. All interlibrary loan requests are sent in standard format via TWX or mail. Requests which resource libraries cannot fill are referred to the RML, which fills all requests it can from within the region, using whatever locator tools it has at its disposal. The RML's and a selected group of other libraries are authorized to refer requests directly to

NLM. Generally, most requests are referred upward, to larger and larger resources.

The hierarchical structure of the network and upward routing pattern for requests means that the collections of the participating institutions serve as a unified, decentralized depository collection of biomedical literature. A user who enters the network at the smallest local hospital library can successively tap greater and greater resources to fulfill his information needs.

The document delivery system of the Regional Medical Library Program is, in its day to day functioning, a relatively unsophisticated operation compared with the computerized MEDLINE services for information retrieval. However, totally without automation, this method of document delivery does work. Last year, the National Library of Medicine alone filled over 150,000 interlibrary loan requests. The RML's and resource libraries filled many, many more. All of this activity was accomplished manually. It is still necessary for human beings to go into the stacks, pull volumes, mail out monographs, make and mail out photocopies, and keep records.

One measure of good document delivery service is speed, that is, minimum turnaround time for filling requests. I just stated that the NLM system does work and has been effective, but I do not believe that I will be giving way any secrets if I say that both we and some of our users would not object if the turnaround time were shorter. I can assure you I spend a great deal of my time being personally involved in the continuing effort to make this process faster, more efficient, and more economical.

The establishment of a national network of lending library depository collections, such as the Association of Research Libraries is considering, may be in order; however, unless we can accomplish major technological improvements in our delivery systems the improvement in the effectiveness of such systems can only be incremental.

I regret that none of us has a ready-made solution. Work is continuing on telefacsimile transmission and on the use of cable television where it exists. Without minimizing the major legal and technical problems inherent in implementing this new technology, our communications experts tell us that high cost is still the major obstacle to overcome. Even so, there have to be more effective methods for obtaining and placing into the hands of a requester those documents he desires. In a real time mode and in response to user's questions, our computerized bibliographic retrieval systems identify for him the articles or books pertinent to his need.

INDONET (A National Computer Network)

INDONET is an integrated information management and distributed data processing facility spanning the country. The primary objective of the project is the establishment of a network of computing centers accessible from remote parts of the country so as to deliver the benefits of information resources management to a wider section of users in the country. This will enable, among others, the predominantly large primary sector as well as industrial and service organizations in remote areas to have access to effective and modern information techniques. This approach would provide an optimal solution to the long-term requirements of modern and sophisticated computing equipment in the country and will prevent indiscriminate and excessive imports of stand alone systems which have been causing a continuous drain on the country's resources; such an approach will also generate an increased demand for indigenous computing equipment (such as terminals, microprocessor based work station, etc.) in the country in larger quantities without which economies of scale are not possible.

Computer Maintenance Corporation Ltd., New Delhi (CMC) is initiating long-term R&D activities to assimilate and indigenise know-how in the field of computer networking in the country. The activities proposed would include development of microprocessor based concentrators, nodal processors and network control processors.

Installation: Communication Links

These computers are being connected by means of P & T voice grade channels (upto 4800 bps) initially. In the second phase, INDONET Computers will be linked via satellite and radio communication. See Fig. 9.1 for inter-city communication links.

Future Plans

The projections by CMC for the Seventh Plan Period, in view of its perceived role in computerization of key sectors of the economy and promotion of contemporary information processing techniques, consider INDONET as a critical vehicle for these activities. The following areas will be enhanced in the next phase (Phase II) of INDONET.

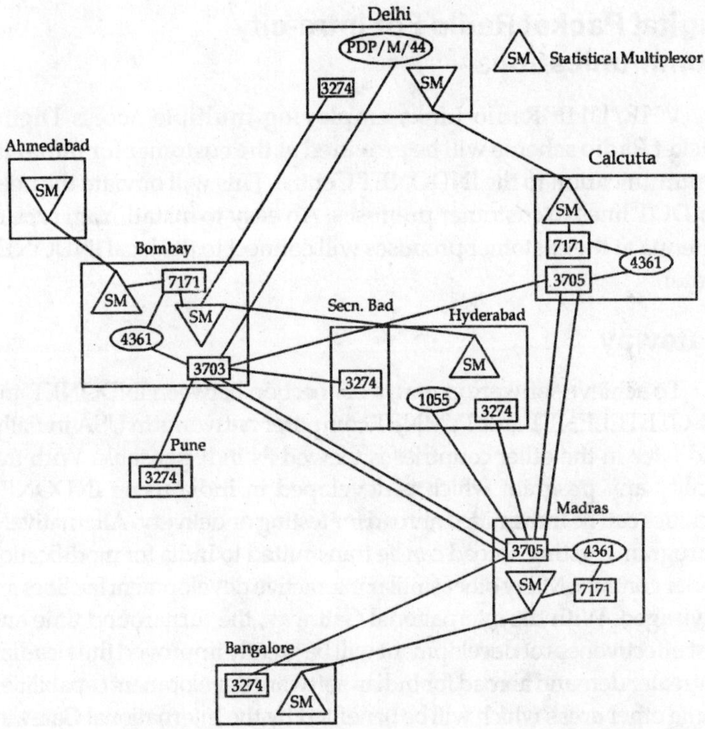

Figure 9.1. Intercity Communication Links

In Phase I, INDONET covers computer centers in 5 cities and three other cities having access points. In the second phase, it is expected that INDONET will cover upto 35 major cities of India.

Satellite Communications

Fast and reliable communication will be provided between INDONET centers through INSAT-IC Satellite links. The bandwidth required will be of the order of $1/5^{th}$ *of a* Transponder Computer and terminals will be able to communicate at speeds up to 9600 bps. The error rate is engineered to be less than 1 in ten million. The INDONET centers will communicate with a

Central Hub through 3 meter Earth Stations. The Hub will communicate through DOT's 11 meter Earth Station, which is already installed.

Digital Packet Radio For Intra-city Communications

VHF/UHF Radio Links employing multiple access Digital Packet Radio scheme will be provided at the customer for intra-city communication to the INDONET Centre. This will obviate the need for DOT lines to customer premises. An easy to install, Yagi type of antenna at the customer premises will connect to the local INDONET center.

Gateway

To achieve software export, a connection between INDONET and the GTETELENET and TYMNET computer networks in USA initially, and later in the other countries is viewed as indispensable. With this facility any program which is developed in India using INDONET facilities can be transmitted abroad for testing or delivery. Alternatively, a program existing abroad can be transmitted to India for modification under contract. Many other similar interactive development facilities are envisaged. With the international Gateway, the turnaround time and cost effectiveness of development will be greatly improved thus leading to greater demand abroad for Indian software development capabilities. Some other areas which will be benefited by the International Gateway are:

1. Foreign Exchange rates will be rapidly available to our banking customers.
2. Rapid distribution of share and commodity prices will assist procurement and export pricing decisions.
3. computer users will have access to databases in USA data banks.

Computers

A super computer at the site of the Central Hub will provide the computing power for the users of the network, in addition to the 5 computers which are already installed in Phase 1. Another super computer is planned for the data bases to be installed on INDONET, considering the storage and computing requirements of the proposed databases.

Databases

Databases installed on the networks abroad (TELENET and TYMNET in US, DATEX-P in FRG and TRANSPAC in France) will be available to the INDONET user through the International Gateway; CMC Limited will provide services as distributor to these databases. In addition, several databases of common interest to Indian computer community are planned to be installed on INDONET systems. They can be shared and accessed by users connected locally/remotely to the INDONET systems.

Numerous packages of industry-standard software are being designed by CMC in different areas. These will be developed on INDONET systems for CMC customers and either run in production mode on INDONET systems, or will be delivered for running on customer/s own systems.

Security

Many of the envisaged INDONET users require stringent control over the security and privacy of their data. To cater to this requirement, a 'least privilege' of 'need to know' policy is implemented for customer data. This means CMC and customer support personnel learn no more about customer data than is necessary to complete the support task. The customer has the option of controlling the level of access. Also a Customer Controlled barrier is provided between his data and all users to protect the secrecy and integrity of the data.

Security Purpose

More specifically, the following measures are implemented for data security:

1. User Identification and Passwords.
2. Encrypted password files.
3. Authorization for Read/Write Execute access privileges to other users.
4. Controlled access to ports and terminals.
5. Time dependent log on configuration.

6. High security transactions from specified terminals only.
7. Physical key option to specified terminals.

Configuration

	Bombay & Madras	Calcutta	Delhi	Hyderabad
CPU	4361-GR4	4361-GR3	PDP-11/44	R-1055M
Memory	4MB	4MB	1.5MB	2MB
Operator Console	One	One	One	One
Disks	3X780MB	3X780MB	2X450MB	(2X200+ 4X100)MB
Tapes	2X1600/ 6250 bpi	2X1600/ 6250 bpi	2X800/ 1600 bpi +2 x 800 bpi	2X1600/ 6250 bpi 3X1600/ 800 bpi
Printer	1200 lpm	1200 lpm	600 lpm	1100lpm +600 lpm
Terminals	10 Local 10 Remote + Users	10 Local + Users	16 Local	8 Local
Comm Contr	3705+3274	3705	3274+Sync. LineInterface DUP-11	3274
PC/AT	2 + 1 Bangalore	1	1	1
AT/370	1 + 1 (Bangalore)	1 +1 (Pune)	1 +1 (Ahmedabad)	1
OS	VM/CMS DOS/VSE	VM/CMS DOS/VSE	RSTS	OS/VS (SVS)

Conclusion

By 1986, INDONET is likely to be the first network of computers in India with the computing power publicly available. The implementation of INDONET is expected to bring about a quality change in the computer applications in India. The second phase of development of INDONET is well under way and a pilot network covering seven cities through Satellite Communication/VHF Radio will be installed by 1986. The extension of geographical coverage of this pilot network to 35 major centers will be taken up next. This will, undoubtedly, provide tremendous challenges and will address the social, technological and promotional needs of the computing community in India.

10

Software for Libraries

Library Computerization in India

Application of computers in libraries has not yet become that common in India as in other countries. But, there is every reason to expect that computers will be increasingly used in Indian libraries during the new decade. Already the necessity and possibilities for utilizing the new information technology for national development are realized by planners and policy-makers in the country. Individual institutions like the BARC, the NIC, the TIFR and the INSDOC could use computers in various housekeeping activities as well as bibliographic information storage and retrieval works. With the advent of more powerful micro computers in the Indian market, the substantial lowering of prices, the liberal financial assistance from funding agencies, and the increased training facilities for librarians, more and more libraries both in the academic and special sectors have initiated action towards computer application. individual efforts by such institutions so far have not made any substantial progress other than successful completion of experiments. One who reviews these experiments will surely come to the conclusion that librarians in India are generally groping in the dark and in need of national guidelines and standardized approaches to the whole question of library computerization. A silver line that has appeared recently amidst the darkening clouds in the sky is the INFLIBNET proposal broughtout by the University Grants Commission. A great amount of work has been done in this connection by bringing together the best brains in the field and by planning the details regarding every aspect of the national library and information which can answer many of the questions that librarians may have in connection with computerization. There is also a promise that as time become ripe necessary standards, guidelines and procedures will be nationally evolved and made available to libraries in the network for uniform application and compliance.

Basic Factors in Computerisation

Computerisation of any library operation involves three basic factors: the hardware, the software, and the peopleware. These are not independent factors. There are not only dependent but also have to be compatible to each other. The hardware will decide to some extent the possibility of using a given software. There are two main types of softwares: The System Software and the Application Software. It is the system software that controls the functioning of the computer and its peripherals. It may contain the operating system, the compilers, the utilities etc. each of which is a programme. Application softwares are made in specific programming languages so as to be run of a specific operating system. This prevents an Application Software made for one operating system from use in another operating System.

Requirement

The above factors should have táken careful scrutiny and adjustments for optimum efficiency at the time of the system study which is a necessary pre-requisite for any library computerisation programme. The major part of this system study is the computer feasibility study carried out by an expert team. Three aspects to be considered here are the technical feasibility, the economic feasibility, and the operational feasibility. The technical feasibility part deals with the computer hardware and other infrastructure. The economic feasibility study is to estimate whether the project would be financially justified. The operational feasibility study is to know whether the project will be user friendly and error free in it's functioning.

Selection of Hardware and its types

The computer system available now can be divided into three: Mainframe computers, mini-computers and micro-computers. The border lines among these are not well defined and it is said that by 2000 we may not have even to differentiate them. Such are the developments anticipated in micro-electronics. Some point out that the discovery of the power in the chip was no less significant than that of the power in the atom. Because it was this discovery that made micro-computers assume the role of minies and even mainframes in recent years. In 1983 it was reported that there were in the United States alone more than 800 models of computers while atleast 200 more were available in other countries such as Japan, Great Britain, Italy, France and Germany. Thus librarians had then more than 1000 models of computers to choose from although all of them were not available in all countries.

Mainframes, Minies and Micros

The difference between the mainframe computers and the mini computers lies mainly in the extent of Main Memory and Backup Memory available, the number of terminals that can be possible for simultaneous use in different operations, the speed of processing obtainable, and the cost involved. Mainframes and minies were popular in the 1970s while the 1980s were mostly of the micros. The first portable micro computer was introduced in 1981 by Adams Osborne. The Original 8-bit micros were soon overtaken by the new 16-bit micros, and in 1983 there were more tan 100 brands of microcomputers in the market. Within another two years the 32-bit super micro was in the market.

Generally speaking, a main frame computer is no more a necessity for a library's requirements, however large and library may be. The choice eventually will have to be between a mini and a micro. With a mini it is possible to store and process massive data at reasonable speed. It can connect a number of work stations enabling inputting, accessing and operating upon data through all of them while the actual storage and processing will be taking place only in the Base System. Another advantage of the mini based computer system is its expandability in terms of its Hard Disk Storage capacity and additional terminals both at lower incremental costs. The mini has also disadvantages. As in the case of the mainframes, the terminals in the mini are not at all independent. The are dump terminals without CPU and, therefore, cannot stand alone. Once the base system is down all the terminals are also down. Another disadvantage with mini is in the matter of system software. Minis are multi-user systems and, therefore, the operating system used will also be multi-user systems and, therefore, the operating system used will also be multi-user ones, like UNIX or XENIX. These are expensive not only in themselves but also in the case of their various compilers, utilities and Application Softwares.

Types of Network

(1) Local Area Network (LAN)

Considering the capacities, convenience and cost on a comparative basis it is found wiser for librarians to go for portable micro computer based systems. Very often, an integrated library operation and management system may require the use of a number of workstations/terminals. This can be facilitated by interconnecting a number of PCs of even different capacities (PC, PC/XT, and PC/AT) into a Local Area Network (LAN). LAN is becoming is becoming more and more popular in India with a number of leading companies marketing the required hardware configurations and the software. Compared to a mini-based system, LAN has several advantages in library application. LAN can have a central File Server with necessary CPU and Hard Disk storage capacity to make care of the massive bibliographic database which is used in common for library operations at different workstations. Added to this the individual workstations may have also other operations to perform. The terminal at each of the workstations is a PC with its own CPU and not just dump terminals as in the case with a mini. This enables these terminals to stand alone even when the File Server or any of the work stations is down. Further, LAN can work in an MS-DOS environment and in effect make the MS-DOS work in a multiuser environment. Ofcourse, LAN software will be an expensive item ranging from Rs. 50,000 to Rs. 90,000. But LAN can eventually bring down the total software costs as a whole since the compilers, utilities and application packages in DOS are generally less expensive than UNIX-based ones.

Software Selection

As mentioned earlier, computer software includes both the system software and application software. The former will be available from the hardware vendor along with the system. But librarians have different options regarding the operating system and its different versions. The factors governing this option are:

(i) The special features or limitations of the hardware. Certain hardwares will function under certain operating systems only;

(ii) The user environment needed-For example, MS-DOS is a single user operating system whereas UNIX and XENIX are multiuser systems;

(iii) The nature of the Application Software to be used-Application packages are made to run under some specific operating system; and

(iv) the cost involved-the prices of operating systems and other system software vary very much. For example today the MS-DOS version 4.0 may cost not more than Rs. 3,500/- while UNIX V3.2 may be ten times that price. Similarly a set of compilers of frequently used programming languages like BASIC, COBOL, PASCAL and FORTRAN under UNIX was quoted for Rs. 40,000 while a set of the same under MS-DOS might be available for not more than half that price.

Selection of Application Software, although not independent of the system software selection, is the most difficult task for the librarian. There are three options for him.

(i) to acquire a ready-made software package;

(ii) to get the software package developed to the order by a software house as a turn key project; and

(iii) to have the software developed locally by himself or his staff. Each of the above has merits and demerits.

Ready-Made Software

Atleast two categories of readymade Library Application Computer Softwares are available-those developed by R & D organizations in library and information field and those developed and marketed by commercial agencies. Generally speaking, softwares belonging to the former category are more dependable than those in the latter. This is because computer personnel in software business houses, without adequate library and information background, will not be that aware of the complexities involved in bibliographical information storage and retrieval. Another defect of the commercially developed library application softwares is that the will lack standardization in descriptive and subject cataloguing of documents which is of primary importance to ensure compatibility with other information systems. Some of the existing standards like the ISBD for books, serials, and non book materials UNIMARK etc. may be often neglected by these packages. On the other hand, software packages developed by library and information personnel with adequate institutional support will have definite advantages over the other category. Coming in the category of softwares having proper institutional support are those available from established library on-line networks to their participant libraries.

Software Development by Order

Local development of the required Application Software either by professional software personnel on a contract basis, or by the librarian or his own staff has more disadvantages than advantages. Not many librarians are good programmers. Moreover, individual libraries should have the required men, money and above all, time to experiment on such projects until their successful completion and fault free application with the desired efficiency and economy.

Individual efforts will only make matters more complicated since there will not be any uniformity or consistency in matters affecting inter-library co-operation. Library automation today has more purposes than putting one's own house in order. The new information technology should enable individual libraries to function as components of larger information system. For this, standardization is indispensable and therefore, libraries individually cannot exercise options outside the national or regional options.

Application Software in India

There are many software houses in India which market library application packages. The UGC Inter-Agency Working group on INFLIBNET is reported to have found not less than 162 packages of various capabilities. Some of the R & D organizations in India that are engaged in activities related to computerization of routine library operations are the Bhabha Atomic Research Centre, Bombay, the Tata Institute of Fundamental Research, Bombay, the Physical Research Laboratory, Ahmedabad, the Indira Gandhi Centre for

Atomic Research, Kalpakkam, Steel Authority of India Ltd., Ranchi, the National Information Centre, New Delhi, the Bharat Heavy Electricals Ltd., Hyderabad, etc. The software modules the have developed cover various library housekeeping operations like acquisition serials control, circulations control, cataloguing and classification, stock maintenance, reference service, inter library loan and on-line bibliographical search and retrieval, SDI services, etc. Besides these, many individual libraries have gone ahead with some project or the other with varying degrees of success.

Requirements of Library Software

1. Libraries have to handle massive data, mainly bibliographical data, which in many respects are different from other textual or numerical data that are usually handled by computers. Hence library application software needs to be specially made for handling large date files innumerable records with unusual record size.
2. The data elements in a bibliographical record will be of varying length. For example, the title of a document may be very short while that of another may be unduly long. The software must meet the situation by providing variable length fields instead of the usual fixed-length fields.
3. Some of the data elements are by nature repetitive. For example, there can be more than one author for a book, and more keywords/subject headings. The software must accommodate such repetitive fields without wasting storage space.
4. Some of the data fields may have to accommodate sub fields also. For example an Imprint Field in a bibliographical record may have to provide for subfields like place, publisher and year.
5. Some of the data elements may not be present in all cases. For example, Collaborator Fields and Series Fields may not be present in some records. The software must have a built in ability to accommodate such optional fields without wasting storage space.
6. Bibliographical data bases should enable speedy random access to files under almost all fields and sub fields. Hence the software should be capable of creating fast access files such as Index files or Inverted files.

7. The speed and efficiency of subject search will depend upon some of the inbuilt mechanisms in the software like the use of a versatile thesaurus management facility, and systematic search languages.

UNESCO – CDS/ISIS Software

A Software package that has been specially made to suit the needs of library computerization is the CDS/ISIS (Computerized Documentation Service/Integrated set of Information Systems). It is developed by UNESCO and distributed by NISSAT in the Department of Science and Technology, New Delhi.

History

The history of CDS/ISIS goes back to 1971 when UNESCO began to be involved in teh development of the information processing software needed for its own newly created Computerized Documentation Service (CDS). Already in the 1960s the International Labour organization had developed a software known as the ISIS (Integrated set of Information Systems). UNESCO sdopted the ISIS of ILO and began to develop the same for use on its IBM Mainframe Computer. The first version of CDS/ISIS came out in 1975. By the end of 1983, after an investment of over 15 man-years in system development, UNESCO brought out the fully developed version 4 of the CDS/ISIS.

A stated earlier, CDS/ISIS was originally developed and conceived as a system for internal use in the UNESCO Secretariat. But it soon become a matter of considerable interest in other countries, especially developing countries, where there were not adequate resources to develop own software or acquire commercially available packages. It has been pointed out that the commercial value of a package comparable to CDS/ISIS is of the order of $100,000 to $1,50,000. Thus UNESCO had to take over the responsibility of developing, maintaining and updating the ISIS/software and of disseminating the same to other international organizations and institutions in Member States.

Latest Version

A subsequent development in this line accomplished by UNSECO has been the Mini and Micro computer version of the

CDS/ISIS which came out in 1986. This version can run on a relatively inexpensive equipment and was developed with a view to help smaller libraries and documentation centers, especially in developing countries, in having access to the computerized information processing technology. The Mini/Micro version can work on IBM compatible Microcomputers running under MS-DOS operating system. The latest version of this software, known as CDS/ISIS Mini/Micro version 2.3, was released in March 1989.

System Overview

The CDS/ISIS Micro Version is a generalized information storage and retrieval system which was designed specially for the computerized management of structured non-numerical data bases containing mainly textual data. The INFLIBNET Inter Agency Working Group reviewed this package as follows. "One of the major advantages offered by the generalized design of the system is that the same set of computer programmes is able to manipulate an unlimited number of data bases each of which may consist of completely different data elements. The user is, therefore, freed from the expensive task of having to design and write computer programmes each time a new project requires the use of information retrieval techniques. Although some features of these packages require knowledge of and experience with computerized information system, once an application has been designed, the system may be used by persons having little or no prior computer experience.

Hardware Requirement

The Mini/Micro version of CDS/ISIS will need a minimum micro computer configuration as listed below:

One IBM-PC/XT or AT or other compatible equipment with 512 RAM Memory (640K recommended)

1. 1 Floppy Disk Unit;
2. 1 Hard Disk;
3. 1 Mono Chrome or Color monitor; and
4. 1 Printer
5. MS-DOS Operating System

Data Base

The package has integrated a number of different programmes into a single program. All these programs are accessible from a main menu. The package allows a *database* to contain over 16 million *records*. Each record can consist of discrete *data elements* that are stored in *fields*. Each field is assigned a numeric *tag*. The unique characteristic of CDS/ISIS is that it is specifically designed to handle fields (and consequently records) of varying length. This feature allows the optimal utilization of the disk storage as well as complete freedom in defining the maximum length of each field. A field may be optional (i.e., it may be absent in one or more records). A field may contain a single data element or two or more variable-length data elements. In the latter case they are *sub-fields* each of which is to be identified by a *subfield delimiter*. Further a field may be repeatable i.e., a given record may have the same field occurring more than once.

Functions

The CDS/ISIS is a versatile package which performs the following functions.

1. Defining the databases containing necessary data elements
2. Entering new records into a new database
3. Modification, correction or deletion of existing records
4. Automatic creation and maintenance of fast access files (index files or inverted files) for each data base in order to maximize retrieval speed.
5. Retrieval of records by their contents from a given data base through a sophisticated search language
6. Displaying the records according to user defined formats
7. Sorting of records in any desired sequence
8. Printing partial or full catalogues/indexes

User Services

ISISENT	Data Entry and Record Editing
ISISRET	Information Retrieval
ISISPRT	Production of Printed Outputs
ISISINV	Inverted File Maintenance and Utility functions

System Services

ISISDEF	Definition of new data bases and/or modification of existing database definitions
ISISUTL	Miscellaneous system utility functions
ISISXCH	Facilities for interchanging data with other systems and Master File utility functions
ISISPAS	Advanced Programming facility for developing own application programs and integrating them with CDS/ISIS

How to Create Database

1. Definition of fields in the records of the Master File using the Field Definition Table (FDT).
2. Definition of Data Entry Work Sheet using the Work Sheet Editor
3. Definition of the parameters for either on-line display of records during searching or for the generation of printed outputs such as catalogues/indexes by using the Formatting Language.
4. Definition of the fields of the data base to be made searchable through the Inverted File by using the Field Select Table (FST) (see fig.4 for a sample FST)

The whole procedure of database creation will be guided and controlled by the Menu System and other interactive features of the package. For instance as soon as you boot in the system and change directly to CDS and ISIS, the main menu appears on the screen with 11 options including the 8 different services listed earlier. Here if you use the command for ISISDEF Service, the menu EXDEF comes upon the screen. You use the appropriate command from the menu EXDEF and you are duly taken care of and guided by the programmes.

Benefits of CDS/ISIS

The advantages of CDS/ISIS Mini-Micro version as a software package specially developed for use in libraries and information centers were already pointed out. Nevertheless there are a few significant plus points more for this software. Firstly, the software is available to libraries free of cost from UNESCO through NISSAT.

Libraries stand to save a considerable amount on this account. Secondly, this is a proven package which is very versatile for our type of work. In the case of other packages they have to be tried and tested for their capabilities. Thirdly, the updating and maintenance of the software is fully guaranteed as UNESCO is its parent body and support. Continued R & D support to Application Software will be normally a costly affair. Fourthly, the software is easy to learn and use. Inspite of that, short term trainings are being widely given in India under the NISSAT manpower development programmes to working librarians in this software. Because of all these, a number of libraries in India have now started working with this software. In Kerala, not much work has been done so far. However, particular mention may be made about the progress made by the Kerala Forest Research Institute, Trichur. This library is reported to have developed in CDS/ISIS 8 data bases covering in all about 16,000 records. Another work of considerable size using this software is the Medical Record Data Base being worked on by Shri C.A. Augustin of the Kerala University Department of Library and Information Science, as one of his research data on 200,000 patient record files available in the Kottiyam Holy Cross Hospital, Quilon. Already 15,000 records have been entered in the data base. Some works are also going on in Institutions like the VSSC Library, Thumba and PSLV Library, Valiamala, the RRL Library, Pappanamcode, and the Kerala University Department of Library and Information Science, Trivandrum. Appears that libraries in Kerala, by and large, do not have to favourable condition for computerization.

Summary

In conclusion it may be pointed out that library computerization is still a long way from this part of India. There is the expectation that during the 1990s, there will be spectacular developments in this field all over India. However, librarians should be prepared to meet the new challenges. They shall have adequate understanding about the hardware and software options available. Individual efforts have to be replaced by co-ordinated and collective national/regional efforts. Otherwise uniformity in matters like the use of Application Software will become impossible. The CDS/ISIS Mini micro version, if accepted for use in all libraries in India, will be a significant step in establishing national uniformity in bibliographical data bases and services.

11

Development of Interlibrary: Loan Service

Growth and Development of Interlibrary Loan Services in India

The first step towards the interlibrary loan system in India was taken by the National Library, Calcutta, when in 1903 it made arrangements for interlibrary loan with the Asiatic Society of Bengal. The first All-Asia Educational Conference was held at Banaras from 26 to 30 December, 1930. In its resolutions delegates requested the inter-University Board of India to bring into operation a scheme of interuniversity library loan of books and bound periodicals, and publish a union catalogue of resources of university libraries in India. The IASLIC Seminar held at Lucknow in October 1964 discussed many important topics of librarianship including inter-library loan services in India.

Mr. Sohan Singh, in his presidential address at the 17th All-India Library Conference held at Indore in December 1968, felt that university libraries in our country have generally an ivory tower outlook and are not sensitive to the ethics of sharing. He advised that "inter-loan services should be in-built in the structure of the University libraries, as 'they are perhaps the best libraries we have in the country and there is no reason why they should confine their services within the university campuses and ignore the larger community in which they find themselves, and they serve as the knowledge-banks of the whole community." More and more libraries statred taking part in interlibrary loan activity. It was felt that active cooperation among libraries was the most important factor in the success of this programme along with reliable and up-to date detailed union catalogue of books and periodicals. Many short union catalogues have been published in India at the national, regional, state, and local level and many are still being published including a few on computers by the Indian Institute of Technology (IIT), Kanpur, and the Indian National Scientific Documentation Centre (INSDOC), Delhi.

INSDOC Document Procurement Centre, New Delhi, supplies, on request, copies of scientific papers in the form of microfilm or photocopy. For this purpose, it draws on the library resources available at the Centre and the libraries in Delhi and other cities. As a last resort, copies of references not available within the country are obtained on microfilm from foreign documentation canters and libraries. INSDOC maintains reciprocal arrangements with a number of foreign documentation centers for getting copies of documents. Thus INSDOC has built up in effect, a large base for the supply of copies of required documents of Indian scientists. This service is being fully utilized by research organizations, universities, industries, and government workers. The service is charged for at a nominal rate so that it is within the reach of most scientific workers. Nearly 20,000 requests for copies of documents are handled every year.

The National Science Library is slightly different in concept. It has been envisaged as more a cooperative acquisition concept, locating materials in places of actual use with only bibliographical control of the holding being maintained through a union catalogue of the Centre. It is an agency to survey the present periodical and monograph holdings in the complex of science libraries in the country and to make good the lacunae by progressively subscribing for materials which, for some reason or other, are not at the moment being subscribed for in the country. The nucleus of the library is functioning since 1964.

To integrate the valuable collections of the science libraries of our country into a single network, availability of up-to-date and dependable catalogues is an essential prerequisite. INSDOC has taken the initiative in the matter and has undertaken a program for compiling the union catalogue of scientific serials. A number of catalogues of serial holdings of major science libraries and a few regional catalogues have already been compiled and published (twelve catalogues so far).

Interlibrary Resources Centres

The disadvantage to the researcher in social sciences is that he has to go from one library to another in search of his material and only in anticipation that the material required by him may become available to him on time in his pursuit of several libraries. In this he faces some odd situations. Many of the Government libraries require special passes to visit them. There are not always good reading facilities provided in some libraries. Most libraries function during normal office hours only and the paucity of staff and space in many of these libraries render the use of the material somewhat difficult for a research worker visiting Delhi for a short period.

A traditional method to this end is the interlibrary loan system. This is a tested method and works fairly well within certain limits. For instance, a few volumes to be obtained or sent on interlibrary loan is not very difficult. It only requires a person to go to another library and get the volumes on loan as well as to return them after use. When the number of such transactions is small and not a daily occurrence, the method of interlibrary loan is cheap as well as quick. But if the transactions are too frequent, difficulties and cost increase concurrently. Different libraries have different rules about loaning their material. Some libraries do not loan periodical volumes as .a matter of rule. Some stipulate that such loaned material must be used on the premises of the borrowing library. The security and care of such material is again a delicate question.

Another method and one of far-reaching significance in terms of sharing resources among several libraries is to establish a center at which different libraries could deposit their infrequently used research material and make this center responsible for organizing this material and providing service to all visiting. scholars.

The Interlibrary Resources Centre is jointly sponsored by the Jawaharlal Nehru University and the Indian Council of Social Science Research. It is concerned with regional centres established at Calcutta, New Delhi, Hyderabad and Bombay.

In setting up the Interlibrary Resources Centre, the Council's objective is not simply to accumulate social science research material at one place, but to provide a variety of services to the community of social scientists among which the following may be mentioned.

To the social scientists who are stationed in Delhi, the Centre is within easy reach. In the course of time, the working hours of the Centre would be extended to facilitate its use for longer hours on working days as well as on Sundays and other holidays.

The Council will also soon provide a reproduction service so that readable photocopies of required articles from periodicals or of reasonable extracts from other documents in the Centre will be supplied on a cost basis to local as well as outside scholars.

The Centre will also maintain a carrier service so that the periodical volumes or documents which are not available in the Centre but are available in some library in Delhi can be obtained on loan for consultation on the premises of the Centre. The union catalogue of social science periodicals and other serials which has already been published will enable the location of periodical volumes in any one of 65 libraries in Delhi.

It is hoped that over the years it would be possible for the ICSSR to establish one regional centre in every major state. It is also proposed to link these centres with the Inter-Library Resources Centre at New Delhi with Telex so that information. about social science research resources could be made available to research scholars and students without loss of time.

The National Library in Calcutta is doing a yeomsn service, to Indian scholars. In fact it has become the main centre of procuring books and periodicals from abroad for research scholars throughout India.

National Lending Library for Science and Technology

The conference of the All-India Library Association held at Delhi, January 17-20, 1976 has recommended the establishment of a national lending library. It would serve as a basis for documentation service as a means for cooperative acquisition of documents and for location of a union catalogue of science. INSDOC now deals with nonbook material service, but for borrowing scientific books it is suggested that a national lending library for science and technology is quite essential. Research libraries in the country can dependably acquire essential material from the proposed national lending library.

In India a great deal of scientific literature is used at present just to a negligible extent. It is because people do not know just what is available where. Abstracting and indexing journals are expensive. Subscription to Russian journals translated into English is also very costly. It must therefore be one of the functions of the national lending library to promote the use of scientific and technological literature. The proposed national lending library can lend to libraries at nominal membership rate basis. This membership fee will cover the postage charges and partly the acquisition of materials. Duplicate copies of material uneconomical to retain on the shelves can be deposited. Appeals to foreign universities, societies, institutions, and trusts for donation of materials will also be fruitful.

National Information System for Science and Technology in India

The "framework" document, of the NCST special panel has identified the following points toward formulation of a national science information policy:

(1) Organization of a national leading library service on the lines of the National Lending Library at Boston, Spain, the United-Kingdom.

(2) Preparation of a national union catalogue of holdings of libraries.

NISSAT will be responsible for coordinating, organising, and providing information at all levels (local, branch, regional, and national). This scheme may be regarded as a landmark in our endeavour to establish a well laid out and coordinated system for science and technology.

Different practices are followed by various libraries which create a great deal of trouble in the way of interlibrary loan. Some lending libraries charge all postal expenses whereas others charge for one way only. Implementation of any scheme of interlibrary loans depends on the framework of rules established by each library institution.

Assessment of the Interlibrary Loan System

The problem is that there is no uniform system yet in the country. The All-India Library Association is taking some steps in the right direction. During the 22nd Annual Meeting held at Delhi in January 1976, a resolution was adopted to make things easy for interlibrary loan. The resolution said, "In view of the fact that the cost of books and journals has increased manyfold.... the facilities for interlibrary loan should be further liberalised and extended to sister institutions. It was further resolved that the postal authorities be requested to reduce the rates for registration and postal charges for material sent on interlibrary. loan from libraries and for this purpose a separate budget head be created in all libraries' budgets."

India is a vast country. The effective interlibrary loan is restricted by the distance between two libraries. Due to the slow postal delivery, sometimes immediate supply of needed material is not possible. It is possible that instead of lending the primary material, future interlibrary loan net-works will transfer photographic and electronic images of primary collections. It is hoped that advances in science and technology in India and the increasing use of telecommunication facilities, computers, reprographics and micrographics by the libraries will make resource sharing and networking more effective and efficient. It is very important that the postal authorities should help us to overcome the problem of delivering the library material rapidly, At the local scene (in big cities and surrounding areas) arrangements should be made by the state or regional library associations to have a daily or three times a week delivery service to deliver interlibrary loan material to all member libraries. A few vans or trucks, with the cooperation of all libraries, can do this job. This system has already been tried successfully in Bombay.

"There are many improvements to be made and we have a long way to go. The librarians responsible for the interlibrary loan service should meet at least once during the annual conference of the All-India Library Association to discuss their problems and find effective solutions to them. Special workshops should be arranged from time to time to guide these librarians and train them in the art of efficiency and better cooperation with other libraries, two most important factors in interlibrary loan service."

12

Document Delivery

The closest competitor of the U.S. Postal Service is UPS, but it is not as accessible as the postal service. Other special delivery systems, for example, Federal Express, are even less accessible and are more expensive. Average delivery time for UPS is two days, and when documents are insured at the same rate, the costs of the U.S. Postal Service and UPS are essentially the same. For photocopies, which do not need to be insured, the U.S. Postal Service is far more economical than UPS as a document carrier.

Boss and McQueen noted in 1983 that 95 percent of the time materials requested through interlibrary loan are sent through the U.S. Postal Service.1k The most important reasons for using this type of mail delivery are availability and cost. Everybody has easy access to the U.S. mail, and special library rates make this method of delivery the least expensive.

Courier systems of a formal or informal nature exist between parent and branch libraries, or if a library belongs to a regional or statewide network, it may be able to participate in a broader-based courier service. Nitecki reports that Illinois, Pennsylvania, and Connecticut library-sponsored document delivery services have one to three days' delivery time with a high degree of reliability.

Library-sponsored delivery services seem to be the least expensive, the fastest, and the most reliable when there is a high volume of activities within a limited geographical area, when a large part of the ILL traffic consists of books rather than photocopies, and when a high degree of reliability in delivery is needed. Turlock reported that in 1986, 73 percent of national multitype library networks had delivery systems linking libraries of the same type and of different types.

Deekle's 1990 article in the *Wilson Library Bulletin* presents an interesting description of the Interlibrary Delivery Service (IDS) of Pennsylvania. It was established in 1969 for delivery of interlibrary loans and other educational materials among its members (academic, public, and school libraries).

Commercial Suppliers

Commercial database suppliers, such as BRS and DIALOG have developed end-user services. DIALOG started in 1972 with two databases. DIALORDER was initiated in 1979 (at about the time OCLC introduced the ILL subsystem) with 14 suppliers. It now has many times that number. BRS began in 1976 with just a few databases. Likewise, it also now has many times that number. Quick ORDER, an *on-line,* on demand, document delivery service for National Technical Information Service (NTIS) documents has been used, especially by special libraries, for many years.

ERIC (Educational Resources Information Center), NTIS, and several other producers offer for sale in microform their document collections accessed through machine-readable databases. CD-ROM disks containing full-text articles may also be purchased.

For a long time database producers have supplied copies of their materials cited in printed indexes and bibliographies. The Institute for Scientific Information, one of the oldest and best known, was the first to be accessible through on-line search services. Deposit accounts are established, and on-line searchers place orders for documents through their terminals. The orders are sent to the database producer, which mails copies to the requesters. DIALOG searchers have access to many database producers and document supply centers, including the British Library Lending Division.

1. British Library Document Supply Service.
2. Center for Research Libraries, Chicago. Primarily for members, but loans are sometimes made to nonmember libraries.

Interlibrary loan librarians should write in advance for information on policies, procedures, and costs.

3. Chemical Abstracts Service. Either documents or photocopies may be obtained. Shipping costs other than first class mail have to be paid.

Dissertations, on-demand books, and serials in microform are also available through the ILL subsystem. Policies and prices are different from clearinghouse items. University Microfilms International has developed a prototype information delivery module; it supports local and remote document retrieval and integrates information searching, ordering, and delivery.

Arthur D. Little's study in 1979 estimated that commercial document suppliers were responsible for about 10 percent of the total document delivery activity and that this percentage was growing at a larger rate than was interlibrary lending among libraries as a whole. In their 1980 report to the Council on Library Resources, Boss and McQueen indicated that 34 percent of special libraries, and more than 10 percent of the nation's academic and public libraries, used nonlibrary document suppliers.

It was assumed by Miller and Tegler that document suppliers must be able to fill a void and supply documents more quickly than libraries were supplying them to one another. To test their hypothesis, they did an analysis of interlibrary loan and commercial document-supply performance.

They compared the performance of commercial document suppliers with the performance of traditional interlibrary loan at the University of Illinois at Chicago. They found that (1) commercial document suppliers are not faster than ILL suppliers; (2) higher charges do not mean faster document supply; (3) local commercial suppliers are no faster than commercial suppliers located at a distance; (4) foreign-language materials, items published before 1970, technical reports, and proceedings do not arrive more slowly or cost more and are not more difficult to supply than current English-language journal articles; and (5) except for engineering, cost, speed, and success rate do not vary by subject area.

Downloading

Downloading from full-text databases offered by BRS, DIALOG, and other commercial systems is another option to consider in document delivery. There are currently more than 1,500 full-text databases available that allow downloading. They are listed in a publication titled *Directory of Online Databases,* which began publication in 1979.

Reintjes found that it is technologically and economically feasible to move the contents of documents electronically among library networks rather than photocopies or the documents themselves. Comparisons were made on response-to-request time, quality of reproduced copy, and cost factors.

Colbert pointed out that disadvantages of full-text on-line retrieval were subscription fees, membership dues, and monthly premiums that must be paid to utilize the on-line services needed for broad coverage, even though she indicated that in many cases, full-text on-line retrieval can be cheaper than hard copy. On the plus side, access to hard-to-find information sources such as newsletters may be obtained on-line. Another advantage is early access. Current information is sometimes accessible on-line before the hard copy is available. On-line is also, in some cases, offering exclusive availability publications because they do not appear in print form. Colbert warns in her "Document Delivery" column in *Online* that in some DIALOG business databases "full-text" can mean an abstracted version of an article or pieces of data abstracted from an article.

A pilot project at the University of Tennessee, Knoxville, January-March, 1989 measured the usage of on-line systems and the cost of obtaining full-text articles electronically. Ninety-one articles were searched for and 83 retrieved for 26 patrons at an average cost of $3.03 per citation with a turnaround time of one to two days.

There are several advantages to obtaining full-text journal articles electronically:

1. A large number of articles may be obtained from one journal without copyright infringement because the articles are purchased with a royalty charge included in the transaction.
2. Electronic retrieval provides faster service than does traditional interlibrary loan.
3. This procedure involves the staff of one library instead of two or more libraries.

There are also some disadvantages in obtaining full-text articles on-line. They are the high cost of searching for incorrect citations and the inability to obtain illustrations electronically.

Downloading requires considerable expertise. In her *Online* column Susan Bjorner discussed ways to minimize the cost of producing full-text output from on-line files when the bibliographic source is known. For each title, the publication *Fulltext Sources Online* lists the systems and databases that contain the source, including dates of coverage. Her own research and research conducted by others indicate that on-line retrieval and printing can be even less costly than commercial document delivery and traditional interlibrary loan because much of the cost associated with the latter two is for retrieval and reproduction labor.

Biblio Data has recently made available three publications regarding on-line, full-text searches. *Online Business Sourcebook,* published in the United Kingdom, also contains some U.S. material. *Newspapers Online is* a directory of daily newspapers. *Fulltext Sources Online* also contains listings of newspapers, as well as newsletters, newswires, journals, and magazines made available by various vendors.

Telefacsimile

The technology of transmitting documents over ordinary phone lines has the potential of revolutionizing ILL document delivery. Telefacsimile, or fax, as it is commonly called, is presently being used for delivery of journal articles. Fax equipment is operated much like a photocopier except that it is also hooked up to a telephone jack.

Fax operates by scanning a page and translating it into tones to be transmitted by the phone, and the tones are, in turn, translated back to dots on a page. Lindberg estimated in 1986 that transmission of a fax took about 20 seconds per page. Many improvements have been made in the technology since that time. One of them is the ability to copy directly from the pages of a book. University of California, Berkeley, library staff, however, expressed disappointment with the direct book-copying feature of the fax machine. The machine performed so slowly that articles continue to be photocopied first and then faxed.

General findings of the study were that 99 percent of the material transmitted was acceptable, with 70 percent considered good quality and 25 percent considered very good quality. Average turnaround time was 2.34 days compared to 10.9 days for postal delivery.

Obviously, document delivery by fax is expensive compared to other types of document delivery. It was pointed out that improvements in machines that prevent having to photocopy articles before they are transmitted and that allow for storing documents in memory and transmitting at a later time would cut down on the greatest barrier to fax delivery. Other advantages and disadvantages pointed out by the Canadian study were : (1) document delivery via fax is instantaneous; (2) fax transmission is ideal for a large network of participants, a high volume of transactions, usage over a lengthy period of time, and when immediate delivery is required; (3) savings in human resources can be realized only if sophisticated enhancements are added to the unit; and (4) E-mail is more effective and efficient than fax for sending messages.

Fax boards installed within a computer are another option for fax transmission. The computer sends and receives the transmissions. The problem that once existed, the inability to run other applications on the computer while faxing, has been overcome.

Images are stored on the computer hard disk until the librarian is ready to print them. Some of the better fax boards, which also cost more money, answer incoming calls and receive and store incoming boxes without interrupting computer work that may be going on at the time.

Anyone interested in setting up a fax network would benefit from an article written by Wilson in the 1988 volume of *Online*. He reported on the experience of Pennsylvania libraries in setting up a fax network. His article also explains how to estimate the cost of fax transmission. He includes the long-distance phone call, personnel costs, and costs of supplies.

Delivery in Universities

In order to enhance faculty research, a number of college and university libraries have begun campus delivery of library documents. The professional literature contains descriptions of the campus document delivery systems developed by several large universities.

After 18 months of the campus book delivery operation at the University of Colorado, 43 percent of the respondents to a 1970 survey (the majority of whom were resident teaching faculty) assessed the service as important or essential to their pattern of use. Sixty-eight percent of the respondents rated the service as excellent; 23 percent rated it as good.

A comparison study of spring quarter 1971 and spring quarter 1972 circulation statistics at Georgia Tech before and after the installation of microfiche catalogs in 35 academic and research departments and the institution of a twice-daily book delivery service showed a statistically significant difference in faculty book circulation Faculty members use the message module of the library's local on-line system to request delivery service to their offices. It has been reported that 90 percent of their requests are delivered within two days.

At the University of Minnesota Twin Cities campus, a document delivery system was considered by those with departmental libraries as helpful by 79 percent and as essential by 15 percent. Those without independent departmental libraries considered the service helpful (66 percent) or essential (17 percent).

A study reported in 1978 at Indiana University, Bloomington, involving 39 political scientists, 14 economists, and 5,478 articles from 620 different journals and newspapers, showed that most articles were supplied by their own library through its delivery service. Nine percent were available through interlibrary loan.

The circulation department of the University of California at Irvine (UCI) began document delivery service in 1986. Circulation staff worked with the campus computing facility to develop an on-line service. A computer program named MELDOC allows users of E-mail to generate requests for delivery of library material, interlibrary loans, MEDLINE materials, and pickup of materials to be returned to the library.

The University of California at Berkeley has developed a fee-based document delivery and bibliographic verification service called Baker. It is available to faculty, graduate students, and staff. Four types of services are offered: delivery of materials to the patron's campus mailbox; verification of citations using local and national catalogs and standard bibliographic works; provision of bibliographic information necessary for requesting through interlibrary loan; and placement of the request with the ILL office, including subsequent delivery of material to the patron. Requests for Baker service are made through E-mail, through campus mail, and by telephone.

Researchers at North Carolina State University can receive journal articles and other library materials via the computers located in their offices, jobs, and research facilities. The Electronic Document Delivery Service (EDDS) automates the entire process of requesting and receiving research materials retrieved from other libraries' collections. There is also investigation under way into the feasibility of delivering library materials electronically between research libraries and across campus networks to the individual researchers. The EDDS includes a mechanism that automatically notifies the researcher through the campus network and retrieves the document. Requests are placed through E-mail. Any type of library information that can be captured in digital form can be delivered over Internet (an international network of networks) and across campus networks to the researcher.

The University of California system, which is composed of nine campuses, is building a prototype system for automating delivery requests that will serve as a model for other systems around the country. A library user will be able to access any document delivery system on the campuses either through the local campus catalog or through the MELVYL (union catalog) system. In addition to setting up standards, the university system is exploring links to commercial document delivery services.

ARIEL, the document transmission workstation (DTW) being pioneered by the Research Libraries Group (RLG), has the potential of streamlining interlibrary loans. ARIEL uses RLG application software with a personal computer, document scanner, and laser printer. Articles from bound journals are scanned into the personal computer, transmitted over Internet to the borrower's workstation, and printed.

ARIEL is similar to the fax machine, but it has several advantages: (1) highquality, high-resolution images printed on regular paper (including fine print, photographs, Chinese scripts); (2) its use of Internet. Many libraries are not being charged for access to Internet, eliminating communication costs; (3) it can store entire documents, which only the most sophisticated Group III fax machines can do; (4) stand-alone fax machines are single-application machines. The ARIEL components can be used for desktop publishing, word processing, scanning, printing, and other ILL operations.

The DTW can be used as a sending and receiving station. When the copyright issues related to electronic storage have been addressed, ARIEL can be used as a scan-and-send workstation for storage facilities or branch libraries, as a print-only station in a branch library or a professor's office, or as a complete scan-send-print workstation in an ILL office.

Home Delivery

Marketing both to the end user and to libraries, Faxon Research Service's Faxon Finder, CARL System's UnCover 2, the RLG's CitaDel, and Lonesome Doc couple journal-citation-level searching with rapid document delivery. Linking citation databases to library holdings streamlines the search process.

The Faxon Finder databases contain more than 11,000 journals covering many subjects. Patrons who search it can then order their articles using Faxon Xpress, Faxon Research Service's delivery service. Faxon Finder may also be searched through OCLC by ILL staff. Faxon Finder promises 24-hour delivery service through fax.

Requests from 12,000 journals can be placed and delivered by fax within 24 hours through CARL's UnCover 2. UnCover 2 is associated with the British Library Document Supply Centre (BLDSC), and in the future, users may be able to order directly from BLDSC.

RLG, which developed the document transmission station called ARIEL, has also developed CitaDel to combine access to commercial and special databases with document delivery direct to the patron. Fax or ARIEL is used for fast delivery.

Lonesome Doc was developed for use in the field of medicine. It also targets the end user by offering citation searching and document delivery. Articles are supplied by participating medical libraries.

Alternative Methods of Delivery

Offprints of articles, especially in the scientific field, are easily obtained from the publishers. Securing offprints for patrons has been an ILL practice for a long time. Issues of periodicals may also be purchased, perhaps eliminating the need for a subscription as well as avoiding the question of copyright.

Herbert White, a library consultant, writes that ILL librarians can do more than simply send a request and then wait, for however long it takes, for a response. He suggests that a quick check of OCLC will sometimes reveal.

Determine whether the material is on the shelf and whether it can be held for an ILL patron, until the proper paperwork arrives. He even suggests the material might be hand-delivered by a colleague. In fairness to ILL librarians, I have known many to go that extra mile for their patrons, actually in much the same fashion as he described it.

13

NICNET (Satellite Based Government Informatics Network)

In the initial stage several doubts were expressed about establishing, a system for providing centralised informatics services. This was mainly because such inter-ministerial projects have not succeeded even in advanced countries. In spite of these apprehensions, a pilot project was initiated in the early phases of NIC's establishment to demonstrate its feasibility based on a computer network. This demonstration was able to clear the apprehensions of the international experts in establishing such a centre in a developing country like India. It was also to some extent able to demonstrate that a high technology based informatics service will provide an economical solution for rapid growth of the economy.

The United Nations Development Programme (UNDP) had provided expertise and relevant hardware equipment and basic software in establishing NIC facilities. During the last four years of its installation, sufficient expertise has been built up at NIC in developing and implementing information systems that could assist the government administration in taking appropriate and timely decisions. Currently, NIC is providing services to more than 50 government departments and has established several information systems in various socio-economic areas. In addition, it has also developed applications that would enable the user ministries to interact with the various databases.

On-line Information for Asian Games

Recognising the expertise built-up at NIC, the Special Organising Committee of the IX Asian Games entrusted NIC with the responsibility to develop an on-line information system for conducting the Asian Games and to provide information on various aspects of the games. This system, in addition to assisting the organising agency in the conduct of the games, provided on-line information about the results, participants and the results of the past major sports events. For provision of such a service, NIC built an on-line information network with 33 terminals spread over a radius of 25 kms at Delhi. The requisite software was developed within a time-frame of 10 months. This modular software took about 30 man-years of efforts. These activities clearly demonstrated the expertise and confidence built up in NIC during the last few years.

As a consequence of these activities, NIC has also evolved a variety of other services and products for increasing efficiency and productivity in the various sectors of the government. All these products have been evolved and developed to improve the services and facilities to the users. The main objective has been in not only developing the system but also facilitating the users to use the system. This had a catalytic effect in organising the data and its usefulness.

Network Growth

With the change in pace of developmental activities and the need to look deep into the resource availability and utilisation, it becomes essential to superimpose on the present information structure, a system and tools for speeding up the process of information collection and compilation. This obviously necessitates a certain, modification on the existing system for introducing modern tools like computers. Further, the existing system not only takes considerable amount of time but also does not have a mechanism of correlating various pieces of data due to non-standardisation of collection and compilation procedures. The present system causes enormous delays, in some case as much as a year. For this purpose, computer becomes very essential in order to reap the fruits of planning in the fastest possible manner.

With the experience gained by NIC in running various systems for central government and projects, it has undertaken for some State governments, it is clear that timely information exchange among agencies involved at various levels in decision-making and implementing is the key to the success of the implementation of various schemes.

For this, it has proposed a project for development of a Satellised Based Government Informatics Network (NICNET). This will ensure a systematic procedure for information exchange among various departments/ministries of the State and Central Governments.

Purpose

The main objectives of the project are:

1. Development of necessary information systems in various sectors of the economy for interactive use.
2. Promotion of informatics at state and national level.
3. Development of monitoring and management methodology for the effective implementation of the projects.
4. Improvement of the analysis capacity and presentation of statistics utilised for regional planning.
5. Development of modelling and forecasting techniques that are required for optimal planning for economic development.
6. Establishment of computer network with necessary communication equipments for ensuring easy access of information across the nation and ensuring optimal use of resources.
7. Development of communication software required for developing governmental informatics network.
8. Development of systems for providing information retrieval on patents, technological developments, production technologies, scientific activities, etc. which are required for fast industrial growth.
9. Become a focal point for on-line accessing of international databases. Evolve and establish facilities for accessing these databases in the most economical manner.

10. Evolving and establishing new network techniques for efficient and economical information service in the government.
11. Development of new methods of investigation and analysis for the improvement of micro-level planning.
12. Development of local expertise in the field of computer-cum-graphical processing of data and micro-level methods of analysis.
13. Evolve standards for data collection, compilation and dissemination, with the cooperation of related agencies at district, State and Central levels.
14. Create a dedicated training school with branches in all parts of the country for extensive training/retraining of existing personnel and users.
15. Research and development in the areas mentioned above and creating necessary infrastructure to develop, operate and maintain the systems.

Features

1. Each District Information Centre will have facilities to collect and compile information that is required to monitor socio-economic developmental activities within that district. In addition, it will also provide facilities to process information that is collected directly by State and Central agencies.
2. Each District Informatics Centre will have a logical communication link with the State Informatics Centre for flow of information among the States and the districts.
3. The State centre will have logical communication links with other State centres, regional centres, and the national centres. This link should support high speed packet data transmission.
4. The network will be reliable and available all the time for efficient information flow.
5. The State, regional and national centre will be capable of sharing load and also serve as back-ups to one another.
6. The National Centre will basically provide computer power to support the information systems of the Central Government.

It will be conceived to support all the government departments with interactive terminals to provide on-line access to the databases. The central system will take the consolidated information system for doing correlative study on the socio-economic aspects relating to the Central plans. In addition, the Centre will have sophisticated research and developmental projects to develop relevant software and hardware tools to support the the district, State and regional activities, and communication hardware and software.

For an effective implementation of the information systems, it is essential that localised computing power be provided at the points (nodes) where either the information is generated or decisions are taken. Such logical points are (a) district headquarters where district level planning is done and actual field information is available, (b) the State headquarters where decisions are taken and project monitoring is done for the entire State.

The regional/national computer systems will have higher computing power to enable all States to operate high computer bound jobs such as for macro planning-like flood forecasting, modelling, etc. It is, therefore, proposed to have a small microcomputer at each district, one super minicomputer system at each State capital and four regional computers to cater to the high computing needs of the country and to have a powerful large mainframe at Delhi.

All these computers at district, State, regional and Central level will be connected in the form of a network permitting free flow of information among these computers and also share the computing load effectively. This is possible with the present day satellite technology. Use of micro earth stations provides a low-cost solution to connect remotely located district computers to the State computer without having to use the leased telephone lines. This gives a reliable computer communication link. This network would provide access of any computer from any location and permit information flow up from district to State and State to Centre and down from Centre to State and State to district level.

Computers on the Network

1. Very large mainframes

   Delhi : NEC S-1000/20D and CYBER 170/730

Pune : NEC S-1000/10
Bhubaneswar : NEC S-1000/10
Hyderabad : NEC S-1000/10
All these systems are expected to be operational by 1986.

2. Interactive terminal (for local as well as global use) in all the above cities.
3. Supermini/Midi computers at State capitals/Union Territories. Terminals will be provided to the users.
4. Computing facilities at all district headquarters.
5. Specialised facilities on the network for CAD, CAM, etc.

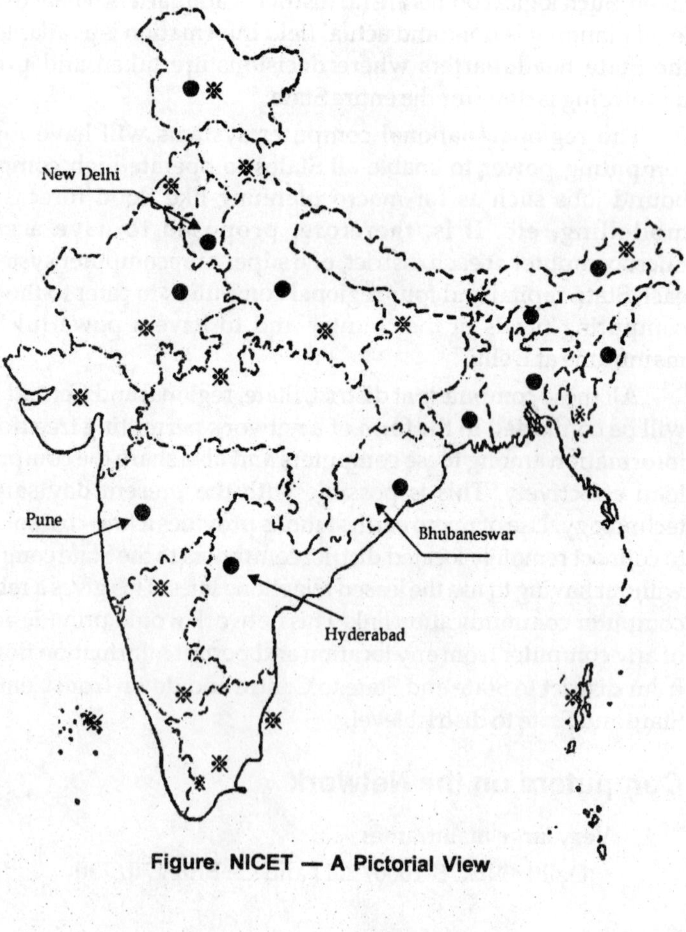

Figure. NICET — A Pictorial View

Impacts

The main impacts of the project will be:

1. Promotion of computer assisted decision-making in government at all levels to improve efficiency.
2. Improvement in overall production through increased availability of information related to agriculture, industry, trade, etc. Generation of increased revenue from sectors like agriculture, industry, trade, etc. Decrease in import for different sectors due to improved productivity within country and thereby saving of huge amount of foreign exchange. Better monitoring, planning and forecasting of the agriculture, industry and trade sectors. Better forecasting for effective planning by providing uptodate and complete data regarding various sectors of the economy.
3. Marked improvement in the management of mass health projects, education schemes, etc.
4. Higher order analysis for meeting the requirements of microlevel planning. The district level microprocessor system will facilitate in predicting rainfall trends, data on demography, village amenities and estimation of growth rates in crop areas.

14

Cyber Reading Rooms in Libraries

Introduction

A cyber reading room is similar to the area of a conventional SLMC where students can go to visit with a friend, read a newspaper, relax with an issue of Seventeen Magazine or Sports Illustrated, practice reading for school play tryouts, meet with an author, participate in a library contest, pick up a bibliography, listen to a book talk or story being read, and much more. It is also place where students and faculty can receive personalized service in the form of reading guidance and suggestions for research assignments. Whether it is the fiction room or the section where fiction books are shelved, this part of the SLMC usually features brightly colored posters, some art prints, a theme-oriented bulletin board/book display, and some comfortable chairs. Its purpose is to provide our users with a non-evaluative environment where they feel thoroughly at ease to ask questions, enjoy themselves, and perhaps take advantage of some special library services and programs.

The introduction of the Internet allows SLMSs to extend the atmosphere, color, services, and programs of the conventional SLMC into cyberspace. For semantic reasons, this area of a school cyber library is called a cyber reading room, but you may wish to call it the Cyber Café, Kid's Room, Cyberia, or sponsor a contest and have the students choose their favorite name for it. Think of it as a place where the programs, services, images, sounds, and sights change frequently. Unlike the Web section of a cyber library that contains links to educational sites, a cyber reading room should furnish links to places that may give a student the "aha!" experience. Make it a site that students will wish to visit more than once and will recommend to their friends.

The Purpose of a Cyber Reading Room

SLMSs and even some administrators may question the need for a school cyber reading room. Is it not the providence of a public library, they may ask? The answer is yes and no. Yes, the local public library should meet some needs of the students in this area, but it cannot personalize its services to the degree that SLMSs can. Unlike public librarians, SLMSs have a more intimate knowledge of the needs and interests of their user population. SLMSs know when a popular teacher is teaching a unit about dinosaurs or reading Charlotte's Web to fourth graders. They can respond more quickly to a heightened subject interest by placing links to dinosaur and/or spider-related sites and read-alike titles for E. B. White's children's classic in a cyber reading room. While public librarians can also provide these activities, they do not have the knowledge of the curriculum and syllabi that enable SLMSs to capitalize on "teachable moments" and the spontaneous enthusiasm that may be generated by an instructional unit or lesson plan.

Most SLMC mission statements contain sentences stating that one of our goals is to meet the educational and recreational reading needs of our students and faculty. Underlying this specific objective is the subliminal message that SLMSs are really attempting to expose students to literature rather than potboilers, to provide them with information in areas that they may be too embarrassed to ask for, and to teach them to be critical users and evaluators of information. Our last unstated, but most important goal is to provide students with such a warm, educationally supportive environment that they will continue to fund, assist, and promote school and public library programs and services in the future. Creating a cyber reading room gives SLMSs an expanded opportunity to fulfill our mission in two important areas.

Cyber Reading Room Opportunity

Before the Internet, if SLMSs were asked to name their biggest competitor for market share of their services, most of us would respond "the television." Students spend an inordinate amount of time watching television-more than they do reading. Children ages twelve through seventeen average about 22.4 hours a week of television compared with 5.1 hours for reading outside of school. Students watch television more than they play with friends and interact with their parents. But now a second competitor to SLMC services and programs has emerged to rival even television for students' time for reading. This competitor is the Internet. Studies show that students are spending more time on the Internet and that it competes with television as a source of recreation. Internet usage studies on the members of the high school class of 2001 found that Internet use has doubled since they were freshmen, from an average of six to eleven hours per week.

Television continues to be a fierce competitor for SLMSs because we do not have access to it. It is an expensive medium in which to create a product and is funded by advertising revenues. SLMSs cannot afford to televise a story hour, host a booktalk, interview an author, or promote new videos or books in this medium because the costs are prohibitive. The medium of the Internet, however, is a different story. This is a medium in which we have, with the exception of the costs of an Internet service provider and a minimal amount of equipment, free access. SLMSs do not have to pay anyone to feature an interview with an author, to link to a new books page, or announce a new library contest or program. We have the unprecedented opportunity to generate content within a medium rivaling our archenemy, television, for students' attention.

Experience Economy

In recent years, economists have emphasized that our economy is service based. The majority of Americans work in jobs that provide a service such as teaching, food delivery, or health care rather than manufacturing something like steel, automobiles, or refrigerators. Economists are beginning to notice a shift from a service economy to one that features experiences. Experience services are distinct from services that individuals purchase when they pick up their dry cleaning or car after it has been repaired. Theatergoers buy an experience when they pay to spend time enjoying a play that a company stages to engage them in a personal way.

Experiences are usually considered the core of the entertainment sector and include drama, concerts, movies, and television shows. In the past twenty years, however, the number of entertainment choices has increased substantially to include many new experiences such as virtual reality, synchronized sound, three-dimensional backgrounds, audio-animatronics, and much more. One of the first people to capitalize on this human desire for experiences was Walt Disney who succeeded in creating a living, experiential cartoon world in California. Disney created the first theme park that not only entertains customers with rides but also immerses them in an unfolding story involving a complete production of sights, sounds, tastes, aromas, and textures. Restaurants are another example of businesses that are part of the experience economy when they not only serve food but also layer on additional sensations with sound, costumed servers, props, and artwork. Children love to visit restaurants such as the Rainforest Café, because they also experience the sights and sounds of rain forests through the use of tropical music and the appearance of live indigenous birds.

While SLMSs can readily identify with the entertainment aspect of the experience economy, we may justifiably question why purchasing a car or even a hamburger needs to be an entertaining experience. Yet publishers have been trying to enhance the reading of our primary product, books, for years through the use of bright book covers, embossed lettering, dramatic photographs, designer fonts, and pop-out art. Preschoolers, for example, have books with pages that simulate a father's beard through the use of sandpaper.

Companies believe that they stage experiences when they engage customers in a memorable way. They are beginning to purposefully use their services as the stage and their goods as props to engage an individual for the following reasons. They know that buyers of experiences, if they are memorable ones, will become repeat customers. If they can make purchasing a car a memorable experience, they hope that you will return to their dealership to purchase another one.

As companies begin to recognize and respond to this subset of the economy, SLMSs have a chance to capitalize on it too by building cyber reading rooms. Our stage is the Internet, our props are books and other information formats, and the experience that we are marketing is reading. Unlike a conventional library that confines many of our goods to a linear format, the Internet provides SLMSs with the opportunity for students to have a sensory reaction to many of our goods and services. Reading a biography of an author can be greatly enhanced by an interview experience with that writer through the Internet. Gazing at the colored plates of famous paintings in an art book can be much more memorable if it is accompanied by a virtual tour of the gallery that actually houses them. Understanding the oral, persuasive powers of Adolf Hitler can be facilitated by viewing a video clip of one of his huge World War II rallies.

Certainly, all of these enhancements could be accomplished in a conventional library, but they would all involve considerably more time, effort, and money to achieve the same effect. Arranging for an author interview entails setting up equipment, class interruptions, rescheduling classes, and an expensive author honorarium. The visit to an art gallery, depending on its location, could involve an overseas visit or, at the very least, a field trip on school buses. With the Internet, it takes only minutes to insert a link to an author interview, art gallery, or historical video clip footage site.

Since we SLMSs have a captive audience for our goods and services for approximately six hours per day, five days per week, many may question the need for making reading more of an experience. Most of us believe that our product-in the form of books, videos, and CDs-is sufficiently attractive to hold student interests and to provide them with memorable experiences. Unfortunately, with the Internet and television claiming much of student free time, this reasoning is complacent and dangerous. While our products are of high quality and content, ours is a service-based profession that needs to offer students and faculty experiences that are memorable or they will search for stimulation elsewhere.

Experience Economy Divisions

Pine and Gilmore, in their book The Experience Economy divide this new economy into four realms, all of which should, whenever possible, overlap. The first division involves the educational aspect of an experience. What do you want students or faculty to learn from the experience that you are providing them? By supplying them with a Webography about dinosaurs, do you want them to acquire more knowledge about dinosaurs' evolution, eating habits, and causes for extinction? What information or activities do the sites provide that might help induce them to explore and learn more about these fascinating creatures?

The second division is the entertainment aspect of the experience. When students are entertained, they are not really doing anything but responding to or enjoying the experience. They may, for example, squeal with delight when they hear a simulation of a dinosaur roar. This part of the site makes the experience more enjoyable so that students will remain at the site to experience the rest of what it has to offer.

The third division is the escapist aspect of the experience and one that SLMSs may consider unnecessary in a cyber reading room. All of us, however, engage in escapist activities. Any SLMS who flies to a professional conference has witnessed hundreds of adults using their laptops to wile away their flight time by playing solitaire. Many others are busy reading the latest formulaic legal thriller by a best-selling author. Students also need escapist experiences. The solution is to choose ones for the cyber reading room that stimulate critical and strategic thinking skills, such as chess or brainteasers, rather than an unchallenging online card game.

The last division concerns the esthetic aspects of an experience. What is it about a cyber reading room that makes students wish to click on it and pass the time away visiting its sites? What can a SLMS do to make the environment student friendly, attractive, interesting, and comfortable? What types of sites in this area would students be most likely to click on again just to experience its contents? For some students, it may be art, for others motorcycles or natural wonders. This is an area where SLMSs have the opportunity to thrill students with something that they have never seen or experienced before.

Cyber Reading Room Content Questions

Although there are a number of standard suggestions and ideas for creating a cyber reading room, each school is in a different location, has unique demographics, and faces diverse technical capabilities. The time and effort that SLMSs spend in designing a cyber reading room also has to be proportional to the other important tasks of operating a SLMC. Before constructing this section of a cyber library, it can be helpful to answer the following questions or pose them to groups of students throughout the school's grade levels.

- For what grade levels will you need to provide sites? Is the age range broad enough that you will need a Children's Room and a Teen Room to attract students?
- Will you provide access to and information about chat rooms?
- Where is the school located? Are there many opportunities for enrichment activities such as field trips to museums, art galleries, foreign travel, live theater productions, and so forth?
- Are there any clubs that could use supporting game sites such as chess or bridge?
- Do you sponsor a conventional book club that could be enhanced by online features?
- What are you technically equipped to provide support for? Can you provide listservs, e-mail activities, multiple-user domains/dimensions, newsgroups, and bulletin boards?
- What do students do for local recreation? Are they close to national parks or outdoor recreational areas?
- How might you address their social interests and possible problems involving dating, friendship, and substance abuse?
- How much of the cyber reading room creation would you be willing to supervise if students indicate that they would like to be more heavily involved in its development?
- When students use the SLMC's terminals in their free time, what sites, games, and other activities hold their attention and interest?
- Is there a population demographic for which a cyber reading room could perform an outreach type of service? Are there students, for example, who leave school early for jobs, have to assume responsibilities for siblings after school, or are not "connected" to the school community?

Cyber Reading Room Size and Scope

While there are no official guidelines concerning the size of a cyber reading room, keep in mind that this is a section of the cyber library that should be responsive to fads, the seasons, current events, and student interests. Sites in this area may be ephemeral in nature because of the subject matter. During the highly contested 2000 presidential election, a cyber reading room may have featured up-to-the-minute news sites about the current status of vote counting in Florida. The second after a winner was declared, those sites should have been deleted.

A cyber reading room is different from a Web library. The latter should be filled with content-rich sites that may not be entertaining but do provide full text about a school-related topic. If there is room, a Web library can expand its collection as long as there is sufficient computer space to store sites and time to maintain them. Although cyber reading rooms do not have a site limit, they should not be an electronic resource that requires multiple subject hierarchies. It should be a place that students and faculty can access quickly for an item or information that is of recent interest.

Subjects within a cyber reading room can reflect the breadth of the fiction area of a conventional library while simultaneously covering student-related interests such as dress and style, the latest music group, and local sports team results. The "quest for the best" is a good motto to follow with a cyber reading room. When Halloween is coming, include only the sites that feature the best costume ideas and pumpkin carving rather than mediocre sites under the rubric "Halloween."

Language in a cyber reading room needs to be hip and informal. Do not be afraid to use the latest student expressions when annotating the sites. The objective is to attract and maintain their interest. Solicit student opinions before choosing a name for this area of a cyber library. If students give it a cool-sounding name, they are more likely to promote it among their peers.

Suggestions for Educational Experiences

While the perfect site contains educational, escapist, entertainment, and esthetic qualities, it is difficult and challenging to find ones that contain all of them. Consider some of these ideas for educational cyber reading room sites. For many students, they will also be entertaining and esthetically pleasing.

1. **Bibliographies:** Bibliography sites can range from a list of new, conventional SLMC acquisitions to theme-related,

annotated lists for either students or teachers. Spark them up with graphics and relevant hyperlinks to other Internet sites for a more sophisticated look. If the school has a color printer, make copies and distribute and display them with the physical books in the SLMC. Keep the last several months in a linked archive for readers who may find time later on to consult them.

2. **Webographies:** Similar to bibliographies, Webographies consist of lists of links that may be really hot for some technical bell and whistle or are subject or theme related. To ensure that students or faculty visit the site, write a catchy annotation to accompany each one. Webographies, unlike bibliographies, provide instant information gratification because users just click to see the contents. If you have prepared one just for faculty members, it may be worth printing and distributing it so that they can bookmark the sites on their own computers.
3. **Book Awards:** Many readers whose time is limited like to read only books that have received some officially recognized form of literary merit. Consider including a book awards site that contains an archive for the Newbery, Caldecott, Booker, Pulitzer, Nobel and National Book Awards.
4. **Book Discussion Groups:** If students are too heavily scheduled to participate in the SLMC's book club, place some links in the cyber reading room to online book discussion groups. Consider placing links to Books@Random Library (http://www.randomhouse.com/library/rgg.html), HarperCollins Reader Resources (http://www.harpercollins.com/readers/reader.resources.htm), or Reading Group Choices (http://www.readinggroupchoices.com/). Perhaps they will have time to join in after school or on the weekends.
5. **Book Reviewers:** Studies have found that students are more likely to seek the advice of a peer than an adult when they need information or have a problem. This same pattern may be true for book recommendations. Consider forming an online book reviewers club of students who are willing to write online reviews for recent, popular fiction. Contact their English

teachers to see if they can receive extra credit and the local school newspaper to see if it will advertise the service and publicize the link address.

6. **Book Reviews:** Students and teachers like to read reviews of books. Many third-generation online catalogs provide links to reviews from professional journals in addition to the annotation to assist readers in choosing titles. You may wish to provide links to the major sites that review materials such as Amazon.com as an extra service.
7. **Booktalks:** These are a wonderful way to promote new titles or introduce students to books that are theme related. They are an integral part of a conventional SLMC's reading appreciation program. Why not provide students with links to some online booktalk sites? There are some excellent ones such as Nancy Keane's Booktalks (http://nancykeane.com/booktalks) that furnish more than mere reviews. These sites can serve as an online readers' advisory site by not only providing additional titles about the same topic but also additional information about the book that is usually not included in typical reviews. SLMSs who have the time may wish to publish their own booktalks online and, if there is some technical support, record them so that students could listen when they click on the titles.
8. **Readers' Advisory:** This is one of the most personalized services that SLMSs offer in conventional SLMCs. It requires that SLMSs read widely in all areas of the collection and be able to retain author and character names, plots, subjects, and themes in the most amazing memory bank: their brains. From all of this mentally categorized reading, they reliably produce books on request about time travel and twins, horses that talk, and kids who run with gangs. While there is no replacement for this type of one-to-one interactive service, some cyber libraries are beginning to establish a similar service via e-mail. Establishing this type of service can be as simple as contacting SLMSs with a written request or posting a form with drop-down menus that help narrow students' choices. Within the Readers' Advisory section, libraries also maintain lists of read-alikes for some of the more popular titles and refer readers to listservs and newsgroups that specialize in

historical fiction, romance, or fantasy. Fiction Mailing Lists (http://www.fictional.org/ralists.html) contains an overview of six popular fiction lists. Students using these lists can lurk until they feel comfortable participating or join in when they want to comment or assist someone else with information. Publishers are also becoming part of readers' advisories by furnishing links to sample chapters, book discussion guides, author interviews, and fan chat rooms. For additional

Readers' Advisory links, refer to Morton Grove's Webrary (http://www.webrary.org?RS/Rsmenu.html)
and

Overbooked (http://freenet.vcu.edu/educaton/literature/bklink.html).

9. **Reading Programs:** Participating in a yearly reading program can be not only educational for students but entertaining as well. If you decide to establish a reading program, this is one area where you need some bells and whistles. Use some reading puzzles, brainteasers, cool graphics, fonts, and bright colors to attract students. Since a reading program takes some time to set up and monitor, be sure to enlist the support of the key school personnel who can help you promote it. Public library sites are more advanced than school cyber library sites in this area because they have historically taken responsibility for summer reading programs. Two programs worth visiting are Oklahoma 2000 Summer Reading Program (http://www.connectok.com/summerfunsite) and Chapter a Day (http://www.chapteraday.com). The former is cosponsored by the Oklahoma Department of Libraries and the Daily Oklahoman newspaper. Its bells and whistles feature audible "mouseovers." Running the mouse over some of the illustrations such as the frog, clock, and snake will produce a croak, tick, and giggle in that order. The site is robust with loads of book lists, book awards, things to do, and more importantly a question-and-answer contest that runs throughout the summer. Chapter a Day is used by 2,700 public and school libraries. It costs approximately 150 dollars for a onetime setup fee. Each weekday, adolescents who enroll in the Chapter a Day Teen Book Club receive, via e-mail, a few pages from the beginning of a popular fiction or nonfiction

book followed the next day by additional pages. Each day's section requires about five minutes to complete answers. By the end of the week, teens will have read about two or three chapters of the book. The following week, they receive a similar amount of content for another book. If you are still debating the idea of a reading program, visit the Florida Library Youth Program (http://dlis.dos.state.fl.us/flyp200) and download a copy of its manual (http://dlis.dos.state.fl.us/bld/FLYP2000).

10. **Relationships:** One of the areas where students, especially teens, need information from reliable sources concerns dating, friendship, and family issues. Within this section, SLMSs may wish to include evaluated links to sites about substance abuse and sex education. The Internet Public Library: Issues and Conflicts (http://ipl.sils.umich.edu/) has an outstanding site under the subject headings Dating and Stuff and Issues and Conflicts that can be mined for ideas and site addresses.
11. **Writing and Publishing Opportunities:** Encouraging students to write and publish their writing has always been one of the most rewarding aspects of a SLMS's job. Many students, however, are either too shy or unfamiliar with our services to request assistance in this area. An online Writing Corner for prose, poetry, and expository writing is a helpful addition to a cyber reading room. The Association for Library Services to Children 700+ Great Sites (http://www.ala.org/parentspage/greatsites/amazing.html) has an excellent resource of eighteen sites under the heading Writing by Children that is worth considering for a cyber reading room.

Suggestions for Entertainment Experiences

Making a cyber reading room an enjoyable area to visit is one of the main reasons for creating it. The competition is stiff for students' viewing hours, and you want students to visit this area of the cyber library as often as possible. Consider linking to sites within these subject areas.

1. **Audio Materials:** Children love to hear SLMSs read and tell stories. Newer computers have the capacity to allow downloading of fairly large audio files without crashing. SLMSs may wish to record story hours and download them

into their cyber reading rooms. If the SLMC's computers can support it, install an audio plug-in so that students can listen to stories during their free time. For ideas, take a look at Toronto Public Library (Canada) (http://www.tpl.toronto.on.ca/KidsSpace/SRC). Its site has an audio file called Books for Me that children can download and sing to because the lyrics are provided on the screen.

2. **Author Interviews and Question Sessions:** Honoraria for authors, even when the costs of their visits are shared among schools, can still be prohibitively expensive. As a policy matter, many authors do not even visit schools. Their publishers, however, are providing Internet sites where they can visit schools electronically. Searching literature portals under an author's name can also yield interviews that have been published on the Internet. Consider creating links to these interviews when students are reading their works as part of a class assignment or just for enjoyment. Investigate the idea of a question-and-answer session with a popular author. Although the publisher may charge for this service and it will never be as personal as a visit, it is not an unworthy substitute.
3. **Cyber Library Contests:** Children like to test themselves, especially when they are in non-threatening situations. While a conventional SLMC may be just the place to host literary or other genre trivia contests, placing it concurrently in a cyber reading room can broaden the audience. If you design a literary contest about famous fictional lovers for St. Valentine's Day, for example, make the game available in the cyber reading room and create a link so that students can send you the answers via e-mail.
4. **Game:** Many SLMCs allow students to play games during the lunch period or after school as long as they are considered educational. For a cyber reading room, you may wish to provide links to similar games that are played in the SLMC such as chess. WebChess (http://www.june29.com/Chess), for example, is an excellent site that provides students with the opportunity to graduate to increasingly more challenging gambits and opponents.

   Mamamedia (http://www.mamamedia.com), however, is the megasite for games. It contains more than 2,000 safe Web sites,

200 of which are replayable activities, including a digital sandbox.

5. **Movies:** On Monday mornings, it is not unusual for SLMSs to overhear students complaining about the poor acting, weak plot, or implausible stunts in a recent movie they paid to see. Students love to go to the movies, but much of their decision to attend is based on television advertising and the recommendations of peers. Why not include in a cyber reading room some links to movie review sites that give them an opportunity to critically evaluate a movie before they part with their money? The Internet Movie Database (http://www.imdb.com/) is one of the best film resources to place in a cyber reading room. It lets students search by title, actor, director, and producer. The plot summaries are lengthy, and movies are classified so that students who liked the latest submarine techno-thriller can find similar ones to rent at their local video rental stores.
6. **Reading Games:** Child development experts are constantly preaching to parents about the need to let children play. Although most of them strongly advocate multidimensional play for children under the age of ten, many children and teens are drawn to computers for play purposes. Providing them with games that involve reading is a much better alternative to having them click on sites that do not stimulate their brains and engage their curiosity. A children's librarian for the Toronto Public Library has observed that games are the most popular part of the library's Web site (http://www.tpl.toronto.on.ca/KidsSpace/SRC). As a result, it has added plenty of them in the form of puzzles and interactive reading stories. Check out its Games and Activities portal site for site addresses, graphics, and other ideas. There are two additional Canadian public libraries with excellent reading games that are worth visiting. Calgary's "Electronic Reading Game" (http://www.public-librar.calgary.ab.ca/wra2000/wra2000.htm) features a multipart Internet game with puzzles and trivia pages about famous Canadians. Students may also search for images in a "Midnight at the Museum" game and keep score on printable score sheets. Interactivity is an important ingredient for reading games because it engages

students' minds. Edmonton Public Library sponsors Bugs in Space/Rocket into Reading that contains an ongoing story about two bug mascots. Players can add new paragraphs, and the best ones are chosen to continue the story's development.

7. **Things to Do:** In this area of a cyber reading room, you may wish to provide visitors with links to events, sites, activities, and happenings within students' more immediate surroundings. If the local newspaper publishes a Weekend Section, this is a good place to start looking for ideas. While you may not find an event's site address, you will probably see a notice giving details as to place, time, price of admission, and so forth. Create a link within the cyber reading room to this information by copying a suitable graphic that expresses the idea of the activity and writing an appropriate blurb about it. If the school is hosting a fall festival, find images or graphics of autumn leaves or pumpkins, create a link to the image, and write a description of the event beside it. Before vacation times, branch out to include sites that students might wish to visit with their parents or relatives including local museums, historic houses, state and national parks, and/or amusement and theme parks.

Suggestions for Escapist Experiences

There is a thin line between entertainment and escapist experiences, but there are differences. Escapist activities usually involve greater immersion than education or entertainment experiences. All of us recognize the signs of an escapist experience when we have to rouse students to run to their next class because they were so engrossed in magazine articles that they forgot the time. One telltale sign of people having escape experiences is the concentration that seems to overcome those persons as they become more immersed in an activity. While all of us dream of this phenomenon occurring with books in the conventional school library, there are many Internet sites that provide a similar experience and are educational in nature.

1. **Cyber Connections:** One of the biggest enticements on the Internet are chat rooms. It's also one of the first Internet activities that was considered unacceptable for students to

engage in during the school day. Students love to talk, share experiences, commiserate, and celebrate with one another. Unfortunately, this Internet activity is such an escapist experience for them that it distracts from learning and completing assignments. Keypals Club, however, which was one of the first tele-computing activities tested online, may be a more acceptable use of the Internet that still allows students to connect with one another in a safe environment. Sites that connect students to one another in foreign countries can assist in sharpening students' reading and writing skills in a foreign language. Geography becomes relevant when students converse with a student who lives in the land they are studying, and everyone benefits from learning what it is really like in a country other than the United States. Keypals Club is available for students of all ages. In some cases, a group of students may correspond with a similar group in a foreign country. Other sites put "pen friends" in touch with one another. EPals (http://www.eplas.com/) is one of the largest sites providing the ability to connect a teacher's classroom with classrooms from ninety countries speaking eighty-seven languages. Its purpose is to arrange for a teacher-monitored opportunity for students to correspond with other students throughout the world. For students desiring a one-to-one exchange, provide them with access to the Keypals Club (http://www.mightymedia.com/keypals/) and show students how to complete the registration instructions.

2. **Interactive Sites:** Sites that provide escapist experiences usually offer a degree of interactivity to engage user interest by allowing them to manipulate information, images, or data and observe the effect it has with other aspects of the site. The site, Amusement Park Physics (http://www.learner.org/exhibits/parkphysics/), for example, lets students move various amusement park rides in certain directions to illustrate different physics principles. Students interested in music would enjoy the Symphony Interactive Guide (http://library.thinkquest.org/22673/index.html) that teaches the components of a symphony by allowing them "to play" different instruments. The census data site Historical United States Census Data 1790-1970 (http://fisher.lib.virginia.edu/

census/) allows students to select ten-year intervals from 1790 to 1970 for each state and county. They may choose up to fifteen variables and request that the data be displayed in various graphs. Another site called Personality: What Makes Us What We Are? (http://www.learner.org/exhibits/personality) gives students the opportunity to take a personality test that helps determine how other people may view them. Highlighting an interactive site within a cyber reading room gives students the opportunity to experiment with it and learn something that might not be part of the curriculum.

3. **Virtual Field Trips:** The world of children can be so narrow because of their geographic location, lack of independence, transportation, and family income. Although they can escape to different countries and even worlds through fiction and nonfiction books, the Internet introduces a level of reality that enhances the experience and makes it more memorable. Discovery sites give students a chance to click on objects, images, and graphics at their own pace and to explore them in more depth. These sites can supplement the book they may be reading on the topic. Parts of the world that are now unsafe or environmentally hazardous can be explored. Places that students have never gone and probably never will can be visited. Highlighting a discovery site in a cyber reading room provides an enriching experience for children and perhaps their parents. Virtual field trips have the potential to inspire students or give them ideas for possible careers. Some virtual field trips are designed to describe particular topics such as how sound waves travel, while others explore sites including ancient Mayan ruins, the Galapagos Islands, and outer space. When inserting a link to a virtual field trip into a cyber reading room, check to see if a teacher is doing a unit in the subject to increase its relevancy and broaden the potential audience. Educational Web Adventures (http://www.eduweb.com/adventure.html) has designed several interactive Internet sites that contain learning modules and Web adventures including Colonial Williamsburg, Weisman Art Museum, the JASON Projects (live satellite and Internet broadcasts of underwater expeditions including the wreck of the Titanic), and the Bell

Museum of Natural History. Virtual School Bus (http:// www.field-guides.com/) takes students to places such as field marshes and volcanoes and contains subject-expert selected sites and pre-cache mechanisms that allow students to download the entire site to their computers and move through at their own pace.

Suggestions for Esthetic Experiences

While an escapist experience is usually characterized by immersion in a site because its offerings are unique and often interactive, an esthetic experience is quite different. Students who have an esthetic experience with a site have little or no effect on it. They leave the site untouched. In a strict educational experience, students learn from entertaining sites they enjoy, escapist sites they visit, and esthetic sites they sense. In the real world, an esthetic experience might consist of gazing at the Mona Lisa or El Capitan in Yosemite National Park or listening to the night sounds in a tropical rain forest. While books can help students imagine some of these places, the old adage "A picture is worth a thousand words" is more applicable. The Internet is filled with sites that give students esthetic experiences. Some of them are sufficiently memorable that they may wish to revisit them.

1. **Art Galleries:** Art galleries abound on the Internet. Almost all of the world's major museums provide gallery like tours of some of their more famous paintings, sculptures, and artifacts. Create a site within the cyber reading room called Painters and Palettes. Insert links to a selected group of paintings from one museum and pose questions about their style, painter, theme, and composition. Tell students what is so remarkable about the work and why it probably came to be displayed in a museum. If time is a factor, just place the site within the cyber reading room, give its details by using a hover button, and have students look at it. Visit the site Art History Sources on the Web (http://witcombe.sbc.edu/ARTHLinks.html) and draw on it for buildings, photographs, and archaeological finds to display.
2. **Exhibits:** Many museums have "blockbuster exhibits" of art, furniture, rare objects, drawings, paintings, scrolls, and so forth that have been collected from various owners and other

museums to form touring collections. Years ago, students only had the opportunity to view these exhibits if their parents took them or if they actually lived close enough to transport themselves to a host city's museum exhibit. Fortunately, this is no longer the case with regard to many exhibits. Through generous funding, many museums mount their big exhibits ontheWeb. The Dead Sea Scrolls (http://www.ibiblio.org/expo/deadsea.scrolls.exhibit/intro.html) and Vatican Museum Exhibit

http://metalab.unc.edu/expo/vaticanexhibit/Vatican.exhibit.html)

can still be viewed on the Internet even though the exhibits have been dismantled and returned to their respective owners and curators. Visit the site WWW Virtual Library: Museums (http://vlmp.museophile.com/) to find ones that are age appropriate and interesting for students to have an esthetic experience that will be truly memorable.

3. **Nature Sites:** Showing students pictures of some endangered species and the world's natural wonders may not only evoke their awe and curiosity but also help maintain their presence on the earth. Without taking the side of the environmentalist or the oil producers, show them pictures, for example, of the Brooks Range and Denali National Park in Alaska. Pose questions that expose them to both sides of the oil drilling issue, or just present them with pictures of Alaskan wildlife, mountains, and valleys to inspire them to take a trip there someday and see it for themselves. Michigan State University has a site called the Children's Garden

   (http://commtechlab.msu.edu/sites/garden/index.html)

   that features more than fifty-six individual theme areas that create a place of wonder and enchantment for students of any age. If your school is in a cold climate, why not link to the site in February when almost everyone has grown a little tired of winter and is awaiting spring?

4. **Web Cameras:** Thousands of Web cameras operate daily on the Internet, but most of us do not associate them with esthetic encounters. Yet these tiny cameras attached to a Web server and automated by software can provide students with many memorable experiences. They can visit a watering hole in

Namibia, Africa, through Noah's Ark at About.com's List of Animal Cams (http://biology.about.com/science/biology/cs/animalcams/index.htm) and watch for antelope and lions to show up. If nothing is going on, they can go underwater to look at the reef in Coral Gables, Florida, or soar to outer space through the satellite images compiled at WebCamVideo.com (http://webcamvideo.com/domi/satel/en.htm). If you wish to access the megasite of web cameras, have them visit Earth Cam (http://www.earthcam.com) for a listing of thousands of cameras grouped into fourteen categories, each with its own subsections. Choices range from gazing at the Acropolis in Greece to searching for killer whales off the coast of Washington State with the orca (killer whale) camera. A second megasite entitled Tony's List of Live Cam Worldwide (http://chili.rt66.com/ozone/cam.htm) provides SLMSs with thousands of possible Web cameras to view and place on exhibit in a cyber reading room.

BIBLIOGRAPHY

A Survey of Generalized Data Management Systems, CODASYL Systems Committee Technical Report, Association for Computing Machinery, New York, May 1969.

A.H. Bobeck and H.E.D, Scobil, "Magnetic Babbles," Scientific American, pp. 78-90, June 1971.

Alan D. Ferguson, "Six Cooperative Libraries," College Management, February 1970, p. 22.

All India Library Conference, 22nd Delhi, 17-20 January 1976. "Resolutions Adopted at the Conference." Indian Library Association Bulletin, 12 (1976), 79-91.

Application of Associative Array Processor to Data Base Management, Goodyear Aerospace Corporation, GER-15260, June 9, 1971.

B. H. Weil, "Document Access," Journal of Chemical Documentation 11, 179 (August 1971).

Banerjea, B.N. "Development of Library Cooperation in india." Herald of Library Science, 3 (1964), 121-126.

C.E. Price, "Representing Characters to Computers," American Documentation, 20(1), 50-60 (January 1969).

Chatteriee, Amitabha. "Problems and Prospectus of Cooperation among the University Libraries in India." Indian Library Association Bulletin, 2 (1966), 69-90.

Computer Output Microfilm, (Auerbach Technology Evaluation Service EDP Series 2), Auerbach Publishers, Inc., Philadelphia, Pennsylvania, 1970.

D. Bishop, "Control and Dissemination of Information in Medicine," in Advances in Librarianship, (Melvin Voigt, ed.), vol. 2, 1971, p. 61.

E. Fong, A Survey of Selected Document Processing Systems, National Bureau of Standards Technical Note 599, Government Printing Office, Washington, D.C., October 1971.

Frederick G. Kilgour, "A Regional Network - Ohio College Library Center," Dalai nation, 16, 87-89, (February 1970).

Frederick G. Kilgour, "Initial System for the Ohio College Library-Center: A Case History," in Proceedings of the 1968 Clinic on Library Application, of Data Processing (Dewey E. Carroll, ed.}, University of Illinois, Graduate School of Library Science, Urbana, 1969, pp. 81-82.

G.G. Dodd, "Elements of Data Management Systems," Computing Surveys 1(2), 117-133, (June 1969).

H.B. Landau, Research Study into the Effective Utilization of Machine Readable Bibliographic Data Bases, Auerbach Corporation, Philadelphia, Pennsylvania, 1969 (PE 184616).

Hakam, Singh. "How to Achieve Optimum Utilization of Existing National Library Resources : Working Paper." Indian Library Association Bulletin, 9 (1973), 90-95.

I.L. Auerbach, "Computer Technology Forecast-1971," presented to IFIP Congress 1971, Ljublgana, Yugoslavia, August 1971.

IASLIC Seminar, 2nd, Chandigarh, 28 September-1 Octobar, 1962. Working Papers and Proceedings, Calcutta: IASLIC, 1965.

International Standard Bibliographic Description: for Single Volume and Multi-volume Monographic Publications recommended by the Working Group on the International Standard Bibliographic Description sot up at the International Meeting of Cataloging Experts, Copenhagen, 1969, 1FLA Committee on Cataloguing, London, 1971, p. iii.

John Phillip Immroth and Jay E. Daily, Library Cataloging: A Guide for a Basic Course. The Scarecrow Press, Metuehen, N. J., 1971.

Joseph Becker and Wallace C. Olsen, "Information Networks," in Annual Review of Information Science and Technology, Vol. 3, (Carlos A. Cuadra, ed.), Encyclopedia Britannica, 1968, p. 304.

Kapoor, S.B.P. "Interlibrary Cooperation in India." Indian Library Association Bulletin, 2 (1966), 105-110.

Kashyap, M.M. "Interlibrary Borrowing Procedure and the Time Taken by the Operation : A Case of Study of the Delhi University Library." Annals of Litrary Science and Documentation, 13 (1966), 204-210

Kumar, P.S.G. Indian Library Chronology, New Delhi: Metropolitan Book Co., 1977.

L. H. Berul, "Document Retrieval," in Annual Review of Information Science and Technology, (C. Cuadra, ed.), Vol.1, Britannica, Chicago, 1969.

Lawrence E. Leonard, Joan M. Maier1, and Richard M. Dougherty, Centralized Book Processing^ A Feasibility Study Based on Colorado Academic Libraries. The Scarecrow Press, Metuchen, N. J., 1969, p. 143.

M. Camras, "Information Storage Density," IEEE Spectrum, 2(7), 98-105 (July 1965),

M.C. Gechman, "Machine-Readable Bibliographic Data Bases," in Annual Review of Information Science and Technology, (C. Cuadra, ed.), Vol. 7, 1972, pp. 323-378.

M.E. Stevens, Standardization, Compatibility, and/or Convertibility Requirements in Network Planning, National Bureau of Standards, Washington, D.C., May 1970 (P B 194479).

N. Lin and W. D. Garvey, "Information Needs and Uses," in Annual Review of Information Science and Technology (Carlos Cuadra, ed.), vol. 7, 1972, p. 10.

Nathan R. Einhorn, "Exchange of Publications," Encyclopedia of Library and Information Science,, Vol. 8 (Alien Kent, Harold Lancour, and William 2. Nasri, eds.), Marcel Dekker, Inc., New York, 1972, pp. 282-289.

National Committee for Science and Technology of India. "Framework for a National Information System in Science and Technology." Paper presented at the Fifth Regional Seminar on Approach to Science and Technology Plan, New Delhi, 21-23 May 1973.

Neelameghan, A. "University Library Resources : Some Observations." Library Herald, 6 (1963), 87-95.

Our College and Universities Today 8(4), (1970-1971).

Patel, F. "Proposal for Inter library Loan among University and Research Libraries." Masters' thesis, Delhi University, n.d.

Patil, P.K. "Interlibrary Cooperation." Indian Library Association Bulletin, 2 (1966), 65-68.

Ronald V. Norman, "The Texas State Library Communication Network Today," Texas Libraries 33 (1971): 42-46.

S. Elspeth Pope, "The Immediacy of Cataloging Information for Newly Acquired Books, " unpublished Ph. D. dissertation, University of Pittsburgh, 1971, pp. 117-123.

Sarah Katherine Thompson, Interlibrary Loan Procedure Manual American Library Association, Chicago, 1970, p. x.

Silvers Willemin, Technique of Union Catalogues: A practical Guide, Unesco, Paris, 1966, p. 6.

T.H. Bonn, "Standards for Computer Networks," Computer 4(3), 10-14, (May/June 1971).

The Bowker Annual, R.R. Bowker Co., New York, 1969, p. 42; 1972, p. 146.

UCLA Librarian, 23(2), 11 (Feb, 1970).

W.C. Jackson, "Telefacsimile at Penn State University: A Report on Operations 1968-69," Library Resources and Technical Services, 15(2), 223-228 (Spring 1971).

Walter Sullivan, "625 Page Book Reduced to Sheet of Microfilm," The Sunday Bulletin (Phila.) Section 1, p, 8, Nov. 23, 1972.

Western Michigan TWX Serves Extension Students," Library Journal 93 (November 15, 1968): 4234.

William J. Welsh, "Report on Library of Congress Plans for Cataloging in Publication," Library Resources & Technical Services, 15, 23-27, (Winter 1971), pp. 25-26.

INDEX